Fearless

Wild Irish Part Four

Vi Carter

Contents

Other Books by VI CARTER

Other Books by VI CARTER

WILD IRISH SERIES

FATHER (FREE)

VICIOUS #1
RECKLESS # 2
RUTHLESS #3
FEARLESS #4
HEARTLESS #5

THE BOYNE CLUB

DARK #1
DARKER # 2
DARKEST #3
PITCH BLACK #4

THE OBSESSED DUET

A DEADLY OBSESSION #1
A CRUEL CONFESSION #2

YOUNG IRISH REBELS

MAFIA PRINCE #1

MAFIA KING #2
MAFIA GAMES #3
MAFIA BOSS #4

MURPHY'S MAFIA MADE MEN
SINNER'S VOW #1
SAVAGE MARRIAGE #2
SCANDALOUS PLEDGE #3

CHAPTER ONE

DARRAGH

"I DIDN'T MEAN IT." My hands sink further into her bloody hair. "I tried to stop it."

Connor stands over me, his chest rising and falling quickly. He moves swiftly toward me. We're now eye to eye as he sits on his haunches.

"Did you hurt her?" His voice is low, but even through my drugged state, I can still hear the threat there.

Shaking my head, I focus on the girl again, who I hold in my hands. "She was dancing and fell."

"Into the pool?"

I blink as I stare up at Connor. "I jumped in and pulled her out, but she won't wake up." I hug the body closer to me. Water and blood mixes around our feet and flows away from us.

"She was smiling." It was just the two of us, a private party, and the drugs kept flowing. First it was me giving her some, cutting it up, but I lost count of how much we took or who was cutting what. "Connor, we had so many drugs." My hold tightens even further on the girl.

"Go back to the house."

I cling to his words and release the girl. A shiver rushes me as I place her carefully onto the floor. I need a fag. The pack sits on the table in front of the couch. I grab them and light one up.

"I owe you one," I say to Connor as I leave.

He doesn't answer me, and I try not to think about what I'm leaving behind.

***

Sweet cookies—that's all I can smell as I move through the kitchen. Throwing my fag into the sink, I search for them and find a tin of cookies on the counter. I stuff two into my mouth and moan in bliss.

Taking the tin with me, I climb the stairs to my room. "You are my sunshine," I sing as I eat the next cookie. "My only sunshine. You make me happy when skies are gray."

I stuff the next one into my mouth and grin. A trail of crumbs is behind me as I enter my bedroom. "You'll never know, cookie, how much I love you. Please don't take my cookies away."

Clutching the tin tighter, I munch on two more, then I fall onto my bed. My hand roams around the tin, looking for more, but they're gone.

"Someone ate all my cookies," I tell the ceiling. My heart pounds as I picture blonde hair coated in blood.

"It's okay," I say to myself as I get up and pull off my wet clothes. "Connor will fix it," I tell myself again as I climb into bed naked. The sheets are cold under me, and my hand searches for the quilt. When my fingers grip the corner, I pull it up over me.

***

I roll and float, my eyes shooting open as my back hits a hard surface. The ceiling looks so far away, and I sit up but quickly close my eyes as my head pounds in pain. I wait until the pain subsides slightly before opening my eyes again. I'm naked on my bedroom floor.

I'm squinting against the throbbing in my head as I search the floor for clothes. Jeans and a T-shirt that smells reasonably clean will do.

The pool house. I need to check the pool house. I'm not sure if I'd been dreaming of a blonde girl. My memory jumps from dancing with her to Connor telling me to leave. No way would Connor have a go after me. It wasn't his style.

I don't bother with socks but put on a pair of brogues as I make my way out to the pool house. The light outside feels harsh, and I dip my head lower. The door is open, and when I enter, nothing looks odd.

Walking around the pool, I'm drawn to the wicker couch at the back of the room. I'm sitting on it, looking around the room, and I'm not sure what I expect to find. My pulse spikes as blood running through the cracks in the tile springs to mind. I'm up and looking behind the couch. But there's nothing, only beige tiles that stare back at me.

"Fuck it." Getting off the couch, I take a few steps to the pool. Turning my back to the water, I grin as I let myself free-fall into the water. My eyes snap open as cold water assaults my body. Rotating, I break the surface and pull myself out. I'm more alert as I walk back to the house.

"What happened?" Mary shakes her head as she stares at the water that drips from my clothes.

"Ah, shit. Sorry, Mary," I say as I pull my T-shirt over my head.

"That's not necessary." Mary sounds flustered, and when I drop my shirt and reach for my jeans, her face flushes.

"I hate wetting your floors, Mary," I say with a smile before I drop my jeans. A scream from her has me pulling the jeans back up. I'm not wearing boxers.

"My bad. I ate all your cookies last night. Can you make me more today?" I lean against the counter and smile up at Mary, but she refuses to meet my eye.

"Yes, Darragh. Just go get dressed."

"Yes, ma'am."

My phone rings when I enter my bedroom. I pull the jeans off. The chaffing from the material has reddened my skin.

"What's up?" I answer.

"Where the fuck were you last night?" DJ asks.

I find clean boxers and yank them on.

"I was going to ask you that. I can't remember. I think I was with a blonde," I say to DJ, pulling on a T-shirt.

His laughter is loud through the speaker. "Yeah, one minute we were chatting, then I go and get a drink and you're fucking gone."

"Well, women before friends," I say.

He snorts.

"I'll catch you later," I tell him. "Going to go feed my belly."

When I enter the kitchen, Mary gives me a quick once-over. Spreading my arms, I do a little twirl. "I'm dressed, Mary."

She smiles. "Sit down, Darragh."

I do as she says. I'm the only one at the table when Una arrives into the kitchen.

"You look rough," she tells me as she gathers up her red hair and clips it high on her head in a way that defies gravity.

"So do you," I say to her, and she sticks her tongue out at me.

"I was in bed early," she says.

I lean across the table. "You might have been in bed early, but I bet my sweet ass you were bumping uglies with shovel face."

Mary swipes at me, and I sit back in my seat. A fry up is placed in front of me. I stand and kiss Mary on the cheek. "I love you, Mary," I declare before I sit down and start to eat.

"Who's shovel face?" Una asks.

I grin and nod. "So you were bumping uglies with shovel face." I stuff half a sausage into my mouth and wink at Una.

Una's face flames, and she starts eating her own breakfast. She glances at the door. "I'm just not having this conversation with you."

I look up as shovel face enters the room. Raising my hand, I wait for a high five. "Una is filling me in on what you guys got up to last night."

He walks past my raised hand and sits down beside Una.

"Ignore him," Una tells Shane as he gives her a kiss on the cheek.

"I always do. But we should let him keep talking. Maybe someday he'll say something intelligent." Shane's words have Una grinning.

"Do you really think so?" Una's enjoying this.

They both look at me, and I focus on my food.

"No, I actually don't." Shane's response is quick.

"How did you even get here? Who let you out of your cage?" I ask Shane, and his shoulders tense. I'm happier now as I munch on my food. Pissing Shane off is such fun.

"Talk to you later, sis," I tell Una as I stand up. Shane's shoulders tighten. "And I suppose talk to you later, brother?" I say it really slowly to let the creepiness of that statement sink in.

Shane levels me with a stare, and I leave the kitchen laughing. *Too easy. Way too easy.*

"Don't forget you start work with Liam," Shane shouts after me, and I pause.

"What, in the brothel?" I ask with laughter in my voice. "Oh God no. Make it stop," I shout as I climb the stairs, and I can hear Una laughing.

***

The silver coating over the painkillers snaps as I gather a handful and wash them down with some coffee. Cars zoom past me, and each one makes my head hurt. I turn into Kells Business Park and drive all the way to the back. Kelly's Kitchens takes up two large warehouses, and I park my car in the front. The smoke from my cigarette blows out around me as I enter the warehouse.

"DJ!" I roar, using my hands to amplify my voice.

He grins at me before offering me a beer. "The cure," he says, and I take it, needing a cure badly.

"What's up, Fitz? I didn't see you around last night." I take the lawn chair that's vacant beside him.

His hood is up, and when our eyes meet, he can't hold my gaze. The lift doesn't go the whole way up with Fitz. He's a mad bastard, so we keep him around.

"My fucking mother found my gun and had a fit. She threatened me with the Gardaí. But I got it back eventually." He stuffs his hands into his white hoodie as he rocks the chair back and forth.

DJ pops open a fresh beer. "Yeah, but she kept his bullets." We laugh as the door opens again.

"How are you drinking again?" Art asks as he saunters over to us like he owns the place. He removes his sunglasses and places them in the *V* of his navy T-shirt. A heavy gold watch shifts as he grips DJ's hand and they half embrace.

"It's just the cure," I say to him, and he shakes his head with a grin.

"Alright, Fitz," Arrt says.

Fitz nods at Art. They have hostility between them. Art is a sneer, and Fitz doesn't like it, but it's never come to blows.

Dragging over a chair, Art sits down. "So, what's the plan?" His brown hair is dipped with highlights. He spends more time on his appearance than most women do.

Lighting a fag, I sit forward as DJ joins us. I wait until everyone is ready before I tell them my plan. I'm smirking with excitement. Already, I can feel the rush.

"We're going to rob an ATM," I say, looking from one to the other. No one looks overly impressed.

"Why? You don't need money."

"Neither do you," I shoot back at Art. He came from money, old money. His well-polished appearance and education makes it questionable why he hangs out with us. I think he likes the chase as much as me.

"So I got word that they'll fill the links close to midnight. We're talking about two hundred thousand, peeps."

DJ's eyes widen, and I've gained Fitz's attention. "We hit around four tomorrow morning. We need to rob a digger to pull it out of the wall, vehicles that we can burn, and a flatbed to take it away."

Art rubs his hands together. "I'm in."

I look at DJ. He removes his cap, runs his hand through his hair, and puts it back on. His vest showcases his tattooed arms.

"Fuck it, I'm in."

Now it's Fitz who won't say no, but we wait, all looking at him. "Yeah, I'm in."

I slap his back, and he grins at me sideways. I finish my bottle of beer. My headache is nearly gone.

"Are we good to bring the ATM back here?" I ask DJ, and he shakes his head.

"Not this warehouse. I have another one. It's small, but I don't want any connection with this one."

"Fair enough." His brothers and father are part of Kelly's Kitchens, so I get him not wanting to tie them into any of this.

"We will need an angle grinder to cut it open."

"I can do that," Fitz offers up.

Why the fuck he has an angle grinder is beyond me. I wouldn't leave him alone with kid scissors.

"So Art, can you steal a Jeep to get us there?"

"You got it, man." Art nods.

"DJ, we'll need to block the street, as well as find a way to get the digger there, which I can get."

He nods. It's a tight schedule to pull this off, but that makes it more exciting.

"So a Jeep and trailer?" he asks.

I nod. "Yeah." That should work. I get myself a fresh drink, feeling happy with the details.

"Any chance of getting a spike strip?" I ask, sitting back down.

"I could make one," Fitz offers up.

Art snorts. "This isn't Metal Work Class 101," he says, but I agree with Fitz.

"Yeah, Fitz, that would be cool. Can you have it here for tomorrow night?" I ask.

He rubs his hands on his tracksuit bottoms. "I can do that."

I raise both eyebrows at Art. "Let's rob a bank," I say and he laughs.

"Heard you had trouble over on your side with the Gardaí," Art says, and the tension in the warehouse seems to rise.

These are my close friends, but they don't know the ins and outs of my family business. "Nah, just someone who tried to get one up on us and failed," I say.

"Heard they were looking for a body." Art focuses on me.

Fitz seems to freeze beside us. We do a lot of dumb shit here, but nothing like what my family does.

"Yeah, they found three," I say. They nod and DJ shifts his gaze to Art. "Three cows," I add before taking a deep gulp of the drink as they all laugh with relief. I'm the kind of guy you just never fully know. I wonder if they actually knew me, would they stay?

"It was a vendetta against my brother, Shane. Some bent cop called it in, but he's pretty red faced now," I say before lighting up another fag.

"So, did you figure out if you pulled last night?" DJ steers the conversation to somewhat safe ground.

"I can't remember, to be honest. Had way too much of the white stuff." Cocaine was too easy of a drug to come by and abuse.

"I picked up a nice little foreign one." Art smirks.

"You tap it?" I ask, throwing my fag onto the ground and crushing it under my boot.

"Yeah, I tapped it." His voice drips with pride, and DJ snorts.

The door opens again. I don't turn around as DJ stands up and walks over to whoever has arrived.

"So what way do we cut up the money?" Fitz asks me, and Art shakes his head at Fitz.

"Equally amongst everyone," I say.

"Fuck no. He has shit for brains. What can he do?"

"Don't be an ass. He'll get a quarter," I say to Art as I place a hand on Fitz's arm.

"Guys, I want you to meet Mark." DJ walks over with Mark, who hobbles toward us on a crutch.

He nods and smiles at everyone, and when our gazes meet, I hope he doesn't recognize me.

Because I recognize him.

CHAPTER TWO

DARRAGH

Mark McGuiness. His name rattles through my head as he nods at me.

"This is Darragh." DJ introduces me, and I stretch out my hand.

"What happened to you?" I ask as DJ drags over another chair and Mark sits down. DJ gives everyone fresh drinks before he joins the circle.

"Got jumped."

"Hate that," Art says. "Is it just your leg?"

I take a deep drink as I listen and tell myself not to fucking smile as I remember my bat, Rochelle, striking his hip.

"I had to get my hip replaced. The fuckers shattered it."

I'm shaking my head. "Animals," I say.

He nods. "When I'm all healed, those fuckers will get what's coming to them." He clicks his bottle with DJ's.

What a fucking moron. "You get a look at them?" I question.

"Nah, the cowards wore masks."

"So how are you going to get them back?" I take a quick drink.

DJ shakes his head at me to leave it alone.

"Yeah, if you don't know what they look like, how will you get them?" Fitz speaks up now. It's like his brain has caught up with the conversation.

"I will. They're lucky my woman and kid were gone. I wouldn't have sat still otherwise."

I snort and shut up as DJ narrows his eyes at me.

"Those dickheads will regret touching you, Mark," DJ says, and Mark clicks his bottle with him again.

"Was it sore?" Fitz asks.

Mark laughs.

"What, my leg?" His question is delivered with a silent word: *idiot*. We can all hear it. Fitz is a fucking idiot. But he's our idiot.

"Yeah, you're fucking leg," I spit out.

Mark eyes me, and I know I should really keep my mouth shut, but I can't seem to help myself.

"Your voice is familiar," he says while rubbing the stubble on his face.

"I have a pretty sexy voice," I say to him with a wink, making Fitz laugh.

"Nah, I've heard it before." Mark frowns at me now.

"Does it really matter?" DJ steps in, looking unsure.

Mark holds up his hands while shaking his head. "Just making conversation, brother."

He isn't DJ's brother. He's too ugly.

"Your voice *is* sexy," Art teases.

"Thanks, Art," I say.

Mark looks awkward at Art's compliment.

"I was once offered a job on those phone sex lines," I say.

"You wouldn't last a night," DJ says, relaxing.

"I know. I would be hunted down and raped," I fire back with a wink.

Everyone laughs, including the muppet, Mark.

My phone rings and I grin. If Mark only knew who was ringing me now.

"What's up, brother?" I ask.

"Where are you?" Connor isn't sounding very friendly.

"Where are you?" I fire back.

"Darragh, I'm warning you," he hisses.

Standing up, I cover the phone. "The woman," I say to the guys and step away. "I'm in Kells."

"Get your ass home now."

"Seriously, what's wrong?"

"I'm not discussing it over the phone."

I light a fag and hang up. "I'm out, guys. See you tomorrow night."

I wave over my shoulder and don't look back as they all say goodbye.

Throwing the fag on the ground, I climb into my car. My head still aches slightly, and I remove a few more painkillers and wash them down with cold coffee.

***

I'm not even through the front door when Connor is on me. He frowns at me. "Where were you?"

"With some friends. You need me to help you with something?" I ask, hoping we get to hurt some people.

He shakes his head.

"Come on." He walks away, and I follow him through the house and out into the yard. Dread tightens around my throat as we walk into the pool house.

"Are you going to ask me about the girl? Because you acting like last night didn't happen is disturbing."

I light up a smoke. "I don't have a clue what you're talking about."

"The girl I had to take to the hospital last night." He walks over to the couch, and my stomach twists. "Or what about all the blood I had to clean up here?"

Flashes of blonde hair covered in blood have me squeezing my eyes, and the memories slowly drip down.

"Ah, fuck. Is she okay?" I ask.

"So, now you remember?" Connor walks back toward me, and I keep the fag in my mouth as I spread my arms.

"I was high," I say, but he follows the ashes that fall from my lips. Removing the fag, I'm tempted to throw it into the pool, but Connor would have a hissy fit.

"She had to get thirty-six stitches in her head. She could have bled to death." Connor is close enough that I smell his cologne.

My stomach curls. I need food. Mary's cookies would be nice. They just dissolved last night. Funny how I remember the cookies.

"Thank God she's okay," I say, but Connor narrows his eyes at me like I'm saying the wrong thing.

"Okay? She's not okay. She got thirty-six stitches." He scratches his jaw. "You need to quit the drugs."

"You need to stop fighting," I fire back.

He rubs his neck and walks toward the bathroom door, waiting for me to join him.

"What the fuck?" I take a step back, but Connor stops me.

"You clean it up."

"Get Mary," I retort, and Connor grips my arm.

"I cleaned up your mess last night. You need to clean this up, and you don't dare ask Mary."

I yank my arm from his. "Fine, I'll do it later."

Connor shakes his head. "Now, Darragh."

"I'm not feeling so good," I say, staring at the bathroom.

Connor nudges me toward the door. There's so much fucking blood, and the bathroom looks like someone wrestled in it. Everything is scattered.

Towels caked in blood lie on the floor, and I step over the first lot of towels. The sink is filled with lumps of what look like bread. I turn my head and gag into my sleeve. Someone got sick in the sink and blocked it. I turn to tell Connor I'm not cleaning it up after all, but the doorway is empty.

He's gone.

Pushing the towels aside, I sit down and light up a fag. I'm trying to piece together what could have possibly happened here last night.

I must have used the towels to stop the bleeding. But the blood on the shower glass? Maybe she flicked her hair and blood splattered across it. Maybe that was already there from something else. She must have gotten sick. I'm not one for puking.

The powder on the top of the toilet is cocaine. We must have had sex, gotten high, and came back in here after she fell.

My phone rings, and I get it out of my pocket.

"You better have that place shining. Heard Michael saying he was going to take a swim later." Connor sounds smug.

"What are you lying for?"

"We'll see." He hangs up and I start cleaning.

We must have used every towel here. The laundry basket is full. I wipe the powder off the top of the toilet and throw my fag into it before flushing. After hosing down the shower and straightening the room, I have only one thing left to do. Clean the sick in the sink.

The toilet brush is in one hand as I face away and swish it around. I hear the water leaking out, and when it's all gone, I'm left with chunks of food. I gag again, and as I turn on the tap, most of it goes down. I get a towel and take out the rest and bin the towel along with a toilet brush.

I ring to the house using the phone in the pool room.

"Hello?"

"Mary, we need fresh towels in the pool house."

"I only stacked them yesterday."

"Yeah, I had a party," I say.

She sighs. "Okay."

"The laundry basket is full. I'll bring it over," I say.

"No. No. I'll do it."

I smile into the phone. "Nice one, Mary. Oh, one more thing. Can you get a new toilet brush?"

"When I'm out later, I'll pick one up."

"I'm going to get you a pay raise," I say.

She laughs and hangs up on me. She's well paid, but I'll slip a good word in for her.

***

"It's all done," I say.

"I'm in the bar having a drink." Connor isn't exactly a day drinker, but I won't refuse.

"On the way," I say as I head into the house.

"You know, I like having you around."

Connor grins. "I think you like me cleaning up your mess, Darragh. But this is the only time I'm going to do it."

"You know you're my favorite brother," I say.

He glances at me sideways while taking a deep gulp of his beer. "I bet you say that to all the girls."

I smirk and pop open a bottle of beer. "I'd murder a fry," I say after drinking half the beer.

"I was serious earlier. I think you should try to stop taking drugs."

The change in topic makes me uncomfortable. So to avoid it, I agree.

"Darragh, you're just throwing away your life."

I force a smile. "You sound like Dad."

"Don't insult me." His hatred toward our dad was never hidden, and it's something that makes me like Connor.

"I can stop. It's just fun," I say as Liam enters, and I know straight away there goes my fun.

"I've been looking for you." Liam walks into the room with his hands in his pockets. Sometimes I question how the fuck we're related.

"You found me," I tell him.

He doesn't grin or frown. Nothing. Nada. I wonder how large the stick is that's rammed up his ass.

"I'm leaving shortly for work, and I think a conversation about rules and such is needed." Liam moves behind the bar, tidies up our caps, and wipes down the small area.

"Would you like another?" he asks Connor.

"Yeah, sure."

He pops the lid for Connor and places it on a mat in front of him.

"What about me?" I ask.

He faces me. "Rules, Darragh. When you're in my establishment, there will be no alcohol, no drugs."

I nod.

"No smoking," he goes on.

I widen my arms. "Nah, Liam, come on."

He doesn't move. "While on your break, you can, but once you're working, it's a no smoking zone."

"Fine, I agree to all of the above." I trace my signature in the air. "You have it signed by air," I say.

"We leave in five." Liam just gives a tilt of his head.

"I can take my own car."

"You're intoxicated, Darragh. You won't be driving today." Liam moves toward the door, and I give his back the finger as he leaves the room.

"Man, I feel like I just got whipped."

"Yeah, you did." Connor smirks at me. "I think this will be fun to watch."

"What? Your brother's misery?"

"No, the rise of Darragh O'Reagan." Connor slaps me on the back as he gets up.

"If I don't come back tonight, Liam has cut me up and stashed me somewhere," I call to Connor, and he just shrugs.

CHAPTER THREE

CIARA

I'VE ONLY JUST STARTED my shift when I realize I need to get a box of gloves. I left a box on my trolley, but they're gone. You want to take your cart home with you or it gets fleeced.

"Hi, Benny."

Benny, who keeps track of inventory, has his head buried in a computer. He glances at me before he returns to his computer.

"What is it?" He taps the keyboard harshly. Friendly as usual.

"I need a box of rubber gloves," I say and he sighs heavily, like the cost of them is coming out of his paycheck. He sits back, giving his stomach a rest from being squashed against the desk.

"Listen, this isn't a free-for-all. You got a box yesterday."

"Yeah, and someone nicked them off my trolley," I say in defense.

"Yeah, yeah, you all say that." He pushes his chair back a ways and rolls to the shelving behind him. I'm praying for a wheel to snap so his fat ass will hit the floor.

No luck.

He rolls back safely with my box of rubber gloves.

Before he hands them to me, his gaze flicks to my hair. "Blue dye isn't allowed."

"Are you discriminating against my hair color?"

He sits up a little straighter. "That's not discrimination." He clutches the gloves to his sweaty chest.

"I was born like this, so it is," I say, and he narrows his already squinted eyes at me.

"No one is born with blue hair."

"Google it," I say, and hope he does on his own time. Luckily, he bypasses his computer and hands me the gloves. I sign for them.

"Nice doing business with you, Benny," I call over my shoulder, but he's buried in the computer again, no doubt Googling if someone can be born with blue hair.

"Boss is here," one of the girls—I can't remember her name—tells me as we pass each other in the hall.

"Thanks." As I turn the corner, I curse my luck. The boss stands at the room I'm meant to be cleaning. A blond-haired guy who looks like he had a few too many drinks is beside him.

"Mr. O'Reagan," I say as I approach.

Liam's gaze snaps to the gloves in my hand, and he gestures for me to enter the room. Fear skitters up my back when the blond guy enters too. Liam knows the drill. I'm a cleaner, and that's it. I flick the blond guy a look as he stares around the room.

"Ciara."

A shiver races across my body at the use of my name.

"This is Darragh, my brother, and he's here to work with you."

Darragh looks like he belongs on some catwalk, not cleaning hotel rooms, especially ones used by prostitutes.

"Okay, I'm not completely down with that," Darragh says. "You want us to be like a double act? I suppose I can do that." Darragh winks at me, and my confusion deepens. "But I won't do men," Darragh adds as he shrugs out of a suit jacket that looks like it cost my yearly salary. "Nor trannies or fatties."

I'm speechless, which isn't something that happens often. Liam closes the door gently behind him, and I take a step back.

"Darragh, you'll be helping Ciara clean the rooms." Liam waits for Darragh to absorb that information.

Darragh's mouth hangs open, and there's something almost comical about it. A part of me wants to walk over and push his chin up.

But I don't. I stay close to the wall, clutching my rubber gloves and praying this will all be over soon.

"Come on, Liam. I could do other jobs. Like help get the newbies to relax." Darragh grins like he's God's gift. "Okay, if that doesn't suit, how about bar work or driving cars? I don't know, but not cleaning. I mean, do I look like a cleaner?" He looks at me like he just remembered I was here. "No offense or anything."

"None taken," I say drily.

"There are no negotiations. If you leave Ciara, she will inform me and there will be consequences." When Liam turns to me, I want to sink into the wall. He has a way of making me squirm without saying a word. "If he leaves and you don't inform me, you're fired."

That isn't fair, but I keep my mouth shut and nod.

Liam gives his brother a final nod and leaves the room before closing the door behind him.

Darragh folds his arms as he chews on a nail, and I know this isn't going to end well.

I start cleaning and my movements snap him out of whatever inner turmoil the poor rich kid was experiencing.

Pulling off the sheets, he jumps back like he might catch something. "Did someone just use that bed?" he asks.

"No, I'm pulling off clean sheets because I don't have enough work," I say in a monotone voice.

He looks at me twice before moving to the wall and sitting on the ground. The ground isn't any cleaner than the bed, but I don't tell him that. It takes forty minutes to put a room back together.

"Now we go to the next room," I inform him.

"I can't believe he's making me do this." He pats his jacket and trousers. "He took my fucking phone."

He's staring at me like I can help him. I can't. I take the dirty laundry and place it under my trolley as I move to the next room. The moment we enter, Darragh goes back to sitting on the ground.

"Are you going to help?" I ask him as I open the curtains.

"Look, no offense or anything, but I don't do this kind of work. I know you women love it, so knock yourself out."

"Wow," I say as I stare down at him. Now I can see why Liam left him here.

I move on to making the bed when he says, "Okay, I found a loophole. Liam said I can't leave you. But you can come with me."

"Genius," I say drily as I start to polish the bedside tables. I'm aware of his movements as he gets up and stands. He towers over me.

"I need a smoke," he pleads.

"Declan, I have ten rooms..."

"It's Darragh." He sounds so offended.

"I have ten rooms to clean before my shift ends. If we leave now, I won't get them finished on time."

"Don't you have breaks?" He sounds appalled.

"Yeah, but not right now."

"But can't you take it right now just this once?" He's smiling at me, trying to charm me.

"Sorry, Derek. No," I say and continue polishing.

"It's Darragh," he says.

I've left the door open, and Darragh hovers close to it. I'm keeping a close eye on him and trying to clean. This is like babysitting a moody toddler.

A brunette is walking past, catching Darragh's eye.

"Hi. You. Come here."

She's also a cleaner, and she smiles up at him as he calls her over.

"Me?" she questions while pointing at herself.

"What's your name?" He places a hand on the doorframe as he stares down at her.

I roll my eyes.

"Mandy."

"Mandy, I'm Liam's brother."

Silence makes me look up.

Mandy isn't smiling. She's walking away.

"No, don't go," he calls after her, but she doesn't stop. "Motherfucker!"

"When's break time?" he asks me.

"Once we do the next room, we can take a twenty-minute break," I say and disappear into the bathroom to clean. When I return, he's sitting on the bed I just made.

"Are we ready?" he asks, standing up.

I straighten the bed behind him before going to the next room. "Maybe if you helped, we could make break time a lot faster."

He snorts. "I'm not from your neck of the woods."

"And where is my neck of the woods?"

He looks me up and down. My mind screams at me to move, but I don't. He shrugs. "You know."

"Actually, I don't," I respond.

He runs his hands through his hair. "You're very lippy for a cleaner."

"You're very lazy for a cleaner," I retort.

He's standing even taller now, shoulders held back. "I'm not a fucking cleaner."

Talking to him is making me want to set my brain on fire. I start cleaning.

"Look, no offense," he says.

"You're fine, David," I respond.

He shifts from one foot to another. "Now I know you're taking the piss." His agitation is growing, and something tells me to stay quiet and just clean, so that's what I do.

***

He's half running down the corridor, pushing the trolley. "Come on, Ciara."

I want to smack him. If it was anyone else, I would be long gone. But when Liam tells you to do something, you just do it.

"Coming," I say sweetly, catching up with him.

"I need twenty smokes."

I open my hand, and he looks at my open palm.

"What?" His brow furrows.

"Money." I want to add the name Drew, but I don't want to push my luck.

"I don't have any on me right now. But I'll give it back."

"You better," I warn him as we reach the locker room. He's hovering over me, and I widen my eyes at him, making him back up. After removing my purse, we head downstairs. There's a fag machine in the hall.

The minute the pack falls into the slot, he reaches to get them.

"Didn't know you could move so fast," I say as he unwraps them.

"Come on." He's already walking away.

"I need to get food," I say.

He tuts. "Get it, then."

He comes with me as I get my fruit out of the small fridge in the canteen. He doesn't speak as we make our way out back.

I'm standing outside with a group of smokers that find Darragh hilarious. I've finished my banana and now move on to my apple. Sitting on the step of a door, I study Darragh and no one notices me.

His humor has picked up, and he's all laughs and smiles, telling tall tales that can't be true. Like how he took on three men at once for hitting on his woman, who he didn't keep in the end. The apple is nearly gone, and Darragh lights up another fag.

"Ticktock, Daemon. Lunchtime is up," I say, and he glances at me like I'm a dog tugging at his trouser leg. I get the attention of the three other guys. They give me a quick once-over, but I don't hold anyone's interest.

I hit the bin easily with my apple. I'm impressed but I'm the only one. One of the guys shivers and glances away, like I did something disgusting.

I walk toward the door.

"Ciara, wait. Just give me one minute," Darragh pleads behind me, but I let the door bang hard so he knows his time is up. I'm only a few steps down the hall when he's behind me.

"Do you have any friends?" he asks, falling into step beside me.

My cat. "Loads. Do you?"

"Of course I do. Look at me." He smirks.

"I am looking at you. So I take that as a no?"

His brow furrows, and he thankfully stops talking.

My job won't be worth doing if I have to work with Darragh every day. I always loved the solitude this job offered, but now it doesn't seem worth the pay.

Darragh rubs his temple. "Do you have any painkillers? My head is pounding."

"I'll check my first-aid kit," I say.

He nods, folding his arms across his chest. He does look a bit pasty.

Once we reach the locker room, I grab my trolley.

"Painkillers," he reminds me.

"I was joking. I don't have a first-aid kit," I say slowly.

"You need to ring, Liam. I'm sick."

"I can't just ring Liam. It's not allowed."

"You can, because I said so."

I'm not comfortable with this, but the idea of getting rid of Darragh has me picking up the staff phone in the hall and dialing Liam's office.

"Mr. O'Reagan."

"Yes, Ciara." I hate how he knows it's me, but then I glance at the cameras in the hall. He must be watching us.

"Darragh is feeling very ill," I tell him.

"Put him on." I hand the phone to Darragh. Time ticks by, and already, I have to shave twenty minutes off my lunch break to get my rooms finished.

Once Darragh puts the phone down, he smiles. "I get to go home."

"With pay?" I ask.

He frowns at me.

"Never mind," I tell him, and push my trolley, making my way to the next room.

It's bliss for the remainder of the day. Sometimes a wrench needs to be thrown into the works to make you appreciate what you already have.

I've come a long way.

My green Nissan Micra sits under a tree, waiting for me to return. I pat the hood before getting in. I live only ten minutes from work—another thing I'm grateful for. Kingscourt is one long strip. Every second shop is closed, but it's become home to me. I park on the street and make my way up to my apartment.

"Hello, Peaches." I pick up my cat as I close the door behind me. Taking her with me, I go into the kitchen and get her a tin of tuna. After taking a forkful first, I scoop the rest into her dish.

I saw Peaches roaming the streets of Kingscourt for weeks before I took her in. No missing cat posters went up, so I claimed her as mine. I knew what being homeless felt like.

I cut up celery, carrots, and parsnips and then boil them before adding some to a stockpot. I have twenty minutes before it will be cooked, so I take the time to shower.

My phone rings in my bag, and I root it out while trying to hold my towel up. The ringtone tells me it's Liam.

"Hi, Liam," I answer.

"Ciara, sorry for the intrusion on your personal time."

"That's okay," I say, tugging the towel closer.

"We've had a problem with a room, and I would really appreciate if you could return and help out. It would be overtime."

"I'll be there in thirty minutes," I tell him. Overtime isn't something I would ever turn down, and he knows that.

"Thank you, Ciara."

"You're welcome, Liam."

I hang up and get dressed. I don't have much time but pour myself a bowl of soup. In the process, I burn my tongue while I scarf it down.

"Be a good girl, Peaches." I rub her behind the ear before leaving.

***

The room is destroyed, but I'm not on my own. One of the other girls is helping me. She's Russian and doesn't speak a word of English, but it's amazing what you can learn from someone just by actions.

The smell of urine is the first thing that hits me. Someone has just sprayed the room. A group of men rented the room, and they sure had a party. The windows are already open, but the mattress is what's holding the smell.

Once I have my gloves on, we pull the mattress off and leave it in the hall. It's picked up within ten minutes, and we start scrubbing the frame of the bed before moving on to the floor. Glass, cans, and cigarette butts litter the floor. How could anyone in their right mind leave a room like this?

I leave the door open, but the smell is still intense, just not as strong as it was before. Laughter out in the hallway has me glancing from where I am on the ground.

Darragh's checking into the room across from me with three girls. They all laugh and smile at him. I shake my head when he pushes open the door and lets them in. His recovery is astounding.

Our gazes meet and I hope my disgust is there, but he winks at me, so apparently it isn't. I want to report him to Liam, but I tell myself this level of irritation over a stranger is unwarranted.

It takes over two hours to scrub the room. My gaze keeps moving to the door across the hall.

"How could he still be at it?" I ask the other cleaner, who stares at me and shrugs while pointing to her mouth.

"No... English."

I wave her off. "Yeah, I know. It's just ridiculous," I say and she shrugs again, repeating herself.

She takes all the dirty laundry out of the room, and I linger a little too long, keeping an eye on the room across from mine. I tell myself I'm dragging it out because it's overtime. That's the only reason I linger for another fifteen minutes before I decide that home with Peaches is where I want to be.

CHAPTER FOUR

DARRAGH

"WHY IS HE HERE?" I angle my head toward DJ.

"Come on, Darragh, he's my mate."

I glance at Mark again. "If he fucks up, it's on you."

"He won't. He'll just be a lookout." I'm not happy with bringing someone else in. Art is bouncing on his feet. He's dressed in black from head to toe, the same as me. Fitz arrives with the angle grinder and the spike strip, dressed all in white.

"Want some?" Art cuts up a few lines, and I grin at him.

"Just what I need." I take the rolled up note and inhale a straight line of powder off a small table. The rush is always instant. I pass the note back to Art as he hits up another one.

I clap my hands together. "Okay, bring it in." Mark's presence is annoying, but for DJ, I'll keep it quiet.

I gesture to DJ. "DJ, you're driving the Jeep with the flatbed. I want you to block Navan road and just stay in the Jeep."

He nods.

"Fitz, your job is to drop the spikes at the end of the Gardaí station. You got it?"

Fitz nods too. But I'm not so fucking sure he's got it. If he fucks up, we can still do this.

"Art, you're the digger driver. You get to take that bad boy out of the wall."

Art yelps his agreement.

"I'll cover you from the road. We have eleven minutes to get in and get out." I look at each person.

"What about me?" Mark asks, and I want to smash his face in.

"You stay with DJ. He's responsible for you." I want him to say something back to me so I can reintroduce him to Rochelle. But he doesn't.

"Once the safe is on the back of the Jeep, we drop it here and then me and Art will get rid of the vehicles while you open the safe." I check my watch. We have five minutes. "Let's do this, bitches."

Art walks beside me, jumping up and down, and we branch off. Fitz takes his own car to go to the police station while DJ and Mark start up the Jeep that has the digger on the back. We let them pull out first. The minute they leave the warehouse grounds, Art and I get into the stolen Jeep and pull down our balaclavas. I fix my black gloves before starting the engine.

I turn on the radio and stop when I come across some dance music. The beat has me pumped as I floor the Jeep down the Cavan Road. Art howls and I laugh.

Yeah, this is going to be fucking epic.

Shivers race all over me with excitement. I love the rush. I love the lack of oxygen and the sensation of chasing air. It's too close to discomfort, but I love it.

I slow down as I approach Kells. No one is around, but I reduce my speed to give DJ a chance to get set up. Art snorts some more coke off his hand and offers me a fresh line that he pours out onto the back of his hand.

"After. I need to keep a clear head," I say.

The steel against my back has my knee jagging. It's loaded and a scary part of me wants to use it. It's a part of me I try to keep a cap on, but it doesn't always work out that way.

I speed up as we come around the bend and approach the bank link. The Jeep and trailer are blocking the road.

"Showtime," I tell Art, spinning the Jeep.

He jumps out and races to the digger. I get out and watch the road. Removing the gun from my trousers, I keep it at the ready. The roar of the digger is going to attract attention.

Three young lads linger across the road, their phones on us. I ignore them as Art drives the digger to the wall. I check my watch. Eight minutes left. The bucket cracks the wall, and debris falls down as Art keeps smashing at the wall around the ATM. The three boys are walking closer, phones held high. My gun rises and they freeze.

"One more fucking step," I warn. I glance at DJ and Mark, who sit in the Jeep. Their focus is on Art as he gets the ATM out of the wall. I want to laugh as he swings the ATM in the air and lands it on the back of the trailer. *Easy fucking peasy.*

I walk back to the Jeep and get in, and Art jumps down from the digger. I wait until DJ has turned the Jeep and drives in front of us. Glancing at my watch, I note that we still have four minutes left.

"You did good, man," I say to Art as I stick her to the road. I have to slow down, but once we leave Kells, I floor it the rest of the way, overtaking DJ. I give him the finger.

Art snorts again. "Ease down, man. We still have to get rid of these vehicles." He rubs his nose and yelps again.

I want to join him, but we need to finish the job first.

After pulling in at the warehouse, we wait. DJ arrives and Art turns the music up full blast and has a fucking party in the back. I focus on DJ as he reverses into the warehouse and tilts the trailer. Once the ATM is inside, I turn down the music.

"You drive this one. I'll take the other," I say to Art.

He climbs into the front, forcing me to get out of the Jeep.

"You know where you're going right?" I ask him.

He blares the music, his head bobbing. I smirk and jump into the other Jeep and take off.

"Fitz, we'll be there in twenty," I say and hang up.

Art drives up beside me, still shaking his head to the music. I push the Jeep harder, not allowing him to get in front of me. He slips back in behind me as another car flashes its lights at him. The minute the coast is clear, he pulls out beside me again. Turning up my own music, I tap the steering wheel before giving him the finger. I push the Jeep to its max. Lights flutter across the hump in the road ahead. Only this time, Art isn't pulling in.

I look at him, and he gives me the finger. I widen my eyes while gesturing to him to fall behind. He gestures at me to move over. My foot is to the floor, and I'm not lifting it.

The car coming toward Art is flashing his lights. I glance at Art again and doubt has entered his features. He pulls in behind me; the car in front jams its breaks on and swerves.

"Wow! Crazy bastard." I'm hyped as I pull into the Lakeside Manor.

The hotel was shut down two years ago, and vandals have smashed nearly every window in the building. I slowly roll down to the water and jump out when the front of the Jeep disappears under the murky water. I'm not even back up when Art pulls into the hotel. Going way too fast, he jumps and hits the tarmac, and his Jeep and trailer go sailing into the water.

"Did you see that?" he roars. "I'm the next James Bond."

"That's the cocaine talking, Art. You wouldn't pull that shit sober," I remind him.

He stands up and wipes grit from his face.

A beat up Toyota slowly approaches us and we jump in. Only then do I remove the balaclava and gloves.

***

"What did I tell you?" I ask the lads as we sit around the bundle of money.

"Nearly two hundred thousand."

DJ looks up at me. I grip his shoulder. "Nice one, Darragh."

Art pats me on the arm. "Yeah, that was some fucking rush."

"So, what way do we split it?" The question comes from Mark, and his voice kills my buzz.

"Evenly?" DJ asks.

"He didn't do anything," Fitz pipes up, pointing at Mark, who rises without his crutch.

I don't move but give DJ a pointed look. He needs to put his friend in his place.

"No. Twenty percent to each of us, and ten percent to Mark." I hate giving him anything.

Mark sits down. "Yeah, that sounds fair."

I don't give a fuck how it sounds. That's just how it's going to be.

"So now can we party?" Art asks, rubbing his hands together. It's like Jekyll and Hyde with Art—once he's worked up, he's loud.

"DJ and Mark, you can get rid of the ATM tomorrow night," I say to them and go for a beer.

I hand Fitz and Art a drink as DJ gets one for himself and Mark.

"We cool?" DJ asks and I nod.

"Yeah, we're cool."

"So how much do I get, like twelve grand?"

I grin at Fitz. "Did you work that out in your head, Fitz?"

He nods.

Mark sneers and I don't fucking like it.

Art takes another line.

"Something funny, Mark?" I quiz.

"I can't seem to sneeze, but you're on my case," Mark states and glances at DJ.

"Let's all calm down and enjoy this. We just robbed a bank," DJ says while pushing his hand into my chest.

"You want one?" Art holds out a note.

"You know I don't like that shit in here, Darragh," DJ whines and I give him both fingers before I walk backward over to Art.

I blink several times after taking the line. "That's good stuff," I say to Art, but he's already bending down for another line. "Did I tell you I got a job?" I say as I walk back to the guys. Lawn chairs are in a circle, and I sit down and light a fag.

"You're working?" DJ asks.

"In a brothel," I tell them.

"No fucking way." Art sits down, wiping his nose.

"Lots of women?" Fitz asks, his eyes wide.

"Yeah, Fitz, lots of women," I say, and he laughs into his hands.

"We need to get him laid," I say to Art.

"Yeah, you need to wet that stick," Art says to Fitz.

"I already have." Fitz sits up straight, all his laughter gone.

"By who?" DJ asks.

I glance at Mark. His smirk is irritating me.

"Well, she turned out to be my cousin."

Art spews his drink on his jeans. "Get the fuck out."

I can't stop laughing.

"She had a massive pair of tits."

I can't breathe. "You're a dirty fucker, Fitz," I tell him and he grins.

"Inbred," Mark mutters under his breath.

I heard him. "Something you want to share?"

Mark stands without his crutch. "Yeah, there is. Every time you speak, your voice just bounces around in my head."

I shrug. "What, am I talking too loud for you?"

DJ stands up. "Darragh, leave it."

I don't even waste a glance at DJ. "Come on, Mark. You want to hit me?" I smirk.

He stretches his arms wide. "Why would I want to hit you?"

"You just look like you do," I tell him. He knows who I am. I can see it in his eyes.

"You came into my home."

I clap. "There we go. Took you long enough."

He rushes toward me, relying too much on one leg. I move quickly and he catches himself before he stumbles and falls. "You're a scumbag."

"Shut the fuck up." DJ pushes him back, but I'm all up for getting shit off our chests.

"Rochelle really liked you," I tell him.

Confusion coats his features.

"My baseball bat," I explain.

He charges again. DJ's grip falters, and Mark rushes me. I'm not a fighter really, but it's too easy. I punch him and it knocks him off balance. He falls on his damaged hip. A roar tears from his lips.

"Darragh." DJ stands over Mark.

"What?" I ask DJ.

"Come on, man. He has one leg."

"Yeah, but he also has a big fucking mouth," I tell DJ.

"Did you beat him up?" Art grins as he swaggers toward me.

"Yeah, while his friend held me down. Coward." Mark just won't keep it shut.

He's still lying on the ground, and I'm tempted to kick him in the face.

"You're the coward, beating up Neill. How many of you jumped him?"

He's standing now. "It was a job."

"So was mine," I say with a grin.

"Nah, you're a sick fuck. You enjoyed it."

His words rub me up the wrong way, and I step closer. "Shut your mouth or I'll reintroduce you to Rochelle."

"You think you're a god," he sneers.

I clench my fists. "I'm a fucking god!" I roar into his face.

He laughs and my blood pounds in my ears. I walk away.

"What are you doing?" DJ asks, still standing beside Mark.

I pick up the canister of petrol.

"Wow, wow." DJ walks toward me, his eyes darting to Mark.

"I'm not going to burn him," I say as I douse the money in petrol.

Everyone is moving, screaming no—all except Art, who is pissing himself laughing.

"I'm your god," I tell Mark, taking the lighter out of my pocket.

"Ah, don't, man," DJ pleads.

Rolling the lighter, a small flame flickers. I don't look away from Mark as he follows the lighter in its free fall as I drop it. His eyes grow wide as all the money goes up in flames.

CHAPTER FIVE

CIARA

"Come on." I wait another few seconds before I turn the key in the ignition. Nothing happens. Resting my head against the steering wheel, I accidentally hit the horn. Startled, I lift my head quickly and stare up at the apartment. I don't know why I'm looking up. No one is going to materialize.

I wanted to go to Carrickmarcoss to do some shopping. That looks like it isn't going to happen. I quickly turn the key in the ignition again, a part of me thinking I can catch the car out. Nope. That definitely isn't happening.

People move along the footpath. I always wonder where everyone is going. At the end, we all end up in the same place. Some of us just get there quicker than others.

Only two years ago, I really thought I would be six feet under. Living on the streets of Dublin is hard. Surviving them was a fluke.

I get out of the car and lock it behind me. No one would steal it, and if they did, I would hug them if they got it started.

The charity shop is at the end of the town. Kingscourt doesn't have an actual clothes store in it, so buying clothes from the charity shop is something I've gotten used to. Large towns and crowds of people make me angsty.

I'm halfway up the street when the skies open and shower down on top of me. I'm not a pessimistic type of person, but I get that shit happens, and it isn't karma or anything like that. It's just life. I've seen firsthand how horrible and cruel the world is, so when the rain soaks right through my shirt, like I'm standing under a waterfall, I don't try to outrun the rain. I just take it one step at a time until I'm standing in the charity shop. The moment I enter, I have to allow my receptors a moment to accept the smell and move on.

I ignore how the shop assistant stares at me as I move around the store. I ignore how the other customers move away if I get too close to them. I want to shake myself like a dog. People piss me off sometimes, but I don't let them get to me. Instead, I ignore them as I browse through the clothes. Two pairs of jeans, a jumper with a small hole in the elbow, and a set of cat ornaments make up my purchase—all costing five euro.

I step back out into the pouring rain. I don't run because it seems pointless. The weather was like this the day I met Liam. I was standing outside the Mater Private Hospital in Dublin. It was always a good spot for begging. Liam, in his suit, walked past me holding an umbrella. I stood there with an empty container. I always kept my money tucked safely in my bra.

"Do you have any change?" I asked with a smile.

"Get a job." His voice was like gravel.

His words had me clenching my hand around my cup. "I would if I could, you asshole."

He stopped walking and looked me up and down before speaking. "I'll give you a job. Come on." He turned away, and I knew I was either walking to my death or to my way off the streets. It was a fifty-fifty. So I took it.

***

Peaches greets me as I enter the apartment. She rubs herself against my wet jeans, then quickly skitters off and jumps onto the couch.

My wet clothes create a pile on the floor as I make my way to the bathroom.

The shower sprays my back. I know it's warm, but it's funny how I don't exactly feel the warmth. My phone rings. I step out of the shower and wrap a towel around myself.

The ringtone for my second job is the sound of someone washing dishes.

"Hello," I answer, trying to keep the phone away from my wet face.

"Hi, Ciara. Would you be able to start your shift early?"

"How early?" I ask Gerard as I walk back into the bedroom. The room is cold and goose bumps break out on my exposed skin.

"The next hour?" Gerard asks apologetically.

I agree and hang up. After getting dressed, I eat a bowl of cereal quickly.

***

One of the new girls rang in sick. In a place like this, it's a rotating door for staff. It's not an easy number. Working for Liam is a lot easier, and if I got more hours, I would give this job up.

The Europa is the most popular chippers in Kingscourt, so once the doors open, it's all go. Right now, I'm washing and peeling spuds until my hands turn red.

Time passes in a blur, and I like the solitude that the back room offers, but that's smashed when Gerard calls me up front to help serve. My stomach rumbles at the smell of all the food.

Gerard takes the orders and calls them to me, so I pack the food and hand it to him. Another guy, whom I don't know, is cooking. He hasn't spoken and neither have I, so it seems like we'll get on.

It's close to one in the morning, and my feet are sore but I'm smiling. It's closing time. The door opens and a group of noisy guys come in. I hunch down further as I tidy over the hot area.

"What can I get you?" Gerard asks.

I throw him a dirty look that he doesn't see. Thankfully.

"Give me a nice breast of chicken," one of the men says.

I roll my eyes as the children start to laugh.

"You're a fucking moron."

I freeze, recognizing the voice.

"I'm not the one with anger problems," says the guy who made the inappropriate comment.

"That's all? Just chicken?" Gerard asks, getting their attention.

"No, we'll order when we're ready." Darragh speaks up again, and I clench my jaw but continue wiping down the surface.

"DJ, you're this close to me hitting you," Darragh says, and the tension in the chippers rises.

I don't know why but I pop my head up. "Still mouthing off," I say without thinking. Everyone looks at me. There's a moment of pure anger from Darragh, but through his drunken state, his eyes widen in recognition.

"Ah, you. The lippy hotel cleaner."

I know Gerard is staring at me.

"You work here, too? Boy, you like cleaning and cooking. A real woman." Darragh winks.

"What can we get you, Darragh?" I ask.

He snorts with humor. "Four chicken breasts," he says with a slow grin. "And can you give me a tub of mayonnaise? You know, since we're friends?"

It's my turn to give a very unladylike snort. "Friends? You'll get the same tub as everyone else." I call the food order out to Gerard and get to work quickly.

"Burn." The guy he called DJ laughs and turns to the other two with them.

One has his hood up. His eyes seem to shoot around the room, and when they stop on me, the feeling leaves me unsettled. He looks like someone's stalker—hooded eyes, hunched shoulders, and his overall presence. The other guy leans against the wall and takes everything in with confidence.

"Shut the fuck up," Darragh shoots off.

I fill the chips at record speed.

DJ points at me. "Didn't think you kept company like that."

I stand straighter. "I want you to leave," I tell DJ, and it's not just him who stares at me, but Gerard gapes.

He tuts like I'm batshit crazy. Maybe I am. The guy leaning against the wall pushes off but doesn't come any closer.

"You'll have to come out here and make me." He grins, and he has every right to. He knows I won't actually make him. He's four times bigger than me.

Gerard calls back to the new guy. "Where's the chicken?"

"Two more minutes." The new guy's accent is foreign. Maybe that's why he hasn't spoken since I arrived. Maybe his English isn't great.

"You heard her. Get out." Darragh speaks up, and I know it's not in my honor. He wants to hit this guy, and I've handed him an opportunity.

"Are you serious?" DJ asks, and the two boys step closer.

I glance at Gerard, and he shakes his head at me, like this is my fault.

I'm surprised when DJ throws the first punch, and it has power behind it. Darragh stumbles back, and the guy in the white hoodie stops Darragh from falling. There's a lull in the chippers as Darragh straightens and wipes blood from his face. A slow smirk grows across his face. I'm waiting and watching for a fight, but Darragh doesn't move.

"That one's free," he says to DJ.

"Hit me back," DJ says, but he sounds afraid now, which makes no sense. He has the upper hand.

"Chicken." The thick accent comes from behind us.

I want to hush him to see what's going to happen next., but Gerard shakes his head before taking the chicken and bagging it.

"I'll hit you back when I'm ready."

"Always playing mind games," DJ shouts and storms away from the chippers.

"Get that, Art," Darragh tells the guy against the wall—the one who reminds me of a stalker. He steps up to the counter with a huge ass grin on his face and pays for the food.

I've seen lots of fights while living on the street, but this one was odd.

Art collects the food.

"See you tomorrow," Darragh sings over his shoulder.

"Yeah, can't wait," I tell him. He won't be fit for much tomorrow. Not that he was helpful the first day either.

Gerard doesn't mention anything after they leave, and we tidy up and shut down in silence.

The next morning, I'm up and getting ready for work, when I remember my car won't start. Taxis aren't exactly parked along the streets here.

I leave my apartment and go to the local shop. Above the phone is a list of all the taxi men in the area, bringing the grand total to two. I ring the first one, and the number is no longer in service. The second one answers and agrees to take me to Tracey's hotel.

After arriving to work and clocking in, I make my way to the first room.

"Hold up."

Turning, I see Darragh in the same clothes as last night—jeans and a baby blue shirt that may or may not match his eyes. He can barely keep those eyes open as he catches up with me; he squints in pain.

"Do you have any painkillers?" he asks the moment he falls into step beside me.

"Let me check my first-aid kit," I joke.

"You know you could be a little nicer to me since I saved you last night."

"Yes, you really taught DJ a lesson."

Darragh's eyes open wider, and a flash of anger storms in them.

My stomach squeezes.

"That's the last time I'll help you out of a hobble." He rubs his head as he speaks.

"I wasn't in a hobble," I say as I push the card into the door handle.

"Fuck's sake, the smell." Darragh covers his nose as he enters the room. "Can't people leave them cleaner?"

"I agree, but I highly doubt you leave hotel rooms clean," I retort as I open the curtains.

Darragh grabs them and closes them. "My head! Just let me get my bearings."

I snort. "We don't have that much time," I say.

He brushes his hand toward me but doesn't make contact. He slides down the wall and sits on the floor, holding his head. I leave him in his cocoon of self-inflicted agony and start cleaning.

CHAPTER SIX

CIARA

DARRAGH'S VOICE STARTLES ME. It's been a while since he's made a sound. I was starting to think he had fallen asleep.

"Do you ever wish you could erase the last five years and start again?"

His question makes me pause. "Why the last five?" I ask. I wish I could erase a lot more than five years.

"Why do you have to answer my question with a question?" He waves his hand in the air, and the motion is so womanly.

"You look gay," I tell him, and he holds his hands wide before pulling them back in.

"What's wrong with you?"

I don't answer. A lot is wrong with me, but telling someone like Darragh my deep, dark secrets would do more damage to my soul than what was already done.

I continue cleaning.

"You look like a dyke with that get up."

I'm wearing the staff uniform. It's two sizes too big, but I like my clothes loose and comfortable. "Maybe I'm a dyke."

"Good fucking chance you are," he shoots back and rubs his temples.

"Are you gay?" I don't even know why I'm asking.

"Did you not see me going into the hotel room with all the ladies yesterday? Because I know you were listening to us."

My face burns, and he laughs at me. He couldn't really know I waited to see if he came back out of the hotel room.

"You're disgusting," I say.

His laughter grows louder. "I know you want me. I see how you look at me."

"You're delusional." I continue cleaning.

He continues sitting there being insulting as hell.

We get three rooms done, and then he wants to smoke. "You owe me twenty euro, and since my car broke down, I need it." I hate explaining myself, but I can't afford not to get my money back.

"Yada. Yada. Yada." He takes out a wallet and gives me a fifty. "I don't want to hear your sob story."

I rip the money from his hand before I slap him and make my way downstairs to the bar.

"We're going that way," he says, pointing in the opposite direction.

I don't stop, and when he grabs my arm, I turn and twist, pushing him against the wall. "Take your fucking hands off me."

He holds his hands in the air and nods. "Okay, calm down."

I release him. The moment I do, warmth rushes my face. He looks at me like I'm crazy.

"I'm going to get your change, and then we can go for a smoke."

"Keep it." He drops his hand and moves away from the wall.

My gaze catches the camera behind us. Damn it. I really hope Liam isn't in the office to witness me assaulting his brother.

I break the fifty, pocket my twenty, and give Darragh his thirty back. We don't speak as we go out back. I sit once again on the step and take an apple out of my apron pocket.

The lads are all over Darragh, but he's subdued. I wonder if I bruised his ego. I couldn't accept someone touching me without my permission. I remember exactly what happened the last time I allowed that.

Once I finish my apple, I stand. This time, I don't have to call Darragh. He's behind me now as we enter the building. I regret defending myself. He watches me, and it's annoying as hell. The hall seems longer today, and I'm glad when we reach the room. The moment we do, Darragh sits back down on the ground.

"Some guy hurt you?" he asks while scratching his head. So my overreaction to him touching me hadn't gone unnoticed.

"Why has it got to be a guy? Maybe a girl hurt me? I'm a dyke, after all." I strip the bed, trying to allow my mind to find that numbness I often feel when cleaning.

"If you want, I can hurt them for you."

The way he says it so offhandedly has my bitch meter rise and hit the bell.

I laugh at him. "Why would you do that? You don't give a shit about anyone but yourself. And honestly, I don't think you'd do very well. I did witness you get your ass handed to you last night, and let's not forget what just happened in the hall."

He grins, but there's no humor in it. "Forget I said anything." He closes his eyes and leans against the wall, and I hate how confused I feel. I can't figure him out for the life of me.

I go back to cleaning, but his response is irritating me. "I wouldn't know where to find him anyway. So it wouldn't matter."

Darragh plays with his lighter when I glance at him quickly. He looks at me and just nods.

"So what about you and DJ? There seems to be a lot of built-up anger there." I don't really expect him to answer, but I want to change the subject.

"I lit his money on fire," he says.

I smirk. What an odd thing to do. "How much?"

"Not sure." His eyes tell me something different, that he knows exactly how much.

"Like a fifty or a hundred?" I'd cry over a fiver. So that amount would make me fall out with someone.

"Yeah, a ton." His answer is quick.

"You could sell your jumper. I'm sure you'd get a hundred for it," I say while straightening out the bed.

"It's not about the money. I could give him his money back. It's the principal."

I'm listening now. "And what's the principal in this case?"

"That I can take anything I want from you. And you can't do anything about it."

I frown and shift my stance. Crossing my arms over my chest, I stare down at Darragh. This arrogant guy is starting to look very dangerous. His party exterior covers up a lot of anger and violence.

"This room is done," I tell him because I don't know what else to say.

We move to the next room. I expect him to leave but he doesn't. He doesn't work either. He just sits and talks until lunch comes around.

I leave my trolley in the room we're cleaning and head to the canteen.

Darragh sticks his head into the canteen, where a few other people sit. "I'm not sitting in there. It's fucking sterile looking."

Several heads turn in our direction. I give an apologetic smile.

Darragh turns away. "I want a steak."

"I have steak. Tuna steak." That's the closest I'd get to steak.

"Come on, I'm not eating in there." Darragh moves away.

"There's nowhere else to eat, Darragh," I say.

He snorts and reaches for my arm but hesitates. "There's a restaurant. We'll eat there."

"I'm pretty sure you can't bring in a packed lunch."

"I'll cover it."

I shake my head. "No."

"You're so awkward. Fine, bring your lunch. I'll sort it."

I grab my food out of the fridge, and it's intimidating as everyone watches me. Darragh taps his foot, and with each tap, I slow down until he stops.

I've never sat inside the restaurant, but I've cleaned it many times. The large crystal chandeliers are a killer to dust. I remember that part clearly.

It's odd being at the opposite side of the table as a waitress steps up. Her eyes linger on me for a second before she turns her attention to Darragh. "What can I get for you?"

He doesn't even look at the menu. "Two steak dinners with chips, and I'll have a Coke." Darragh turns to me, and I shake my head. "Make that two Cokes," he tells the waitress, who then disappears.

"I told you I have lunch," I say, patting my food beside me.

"Don't take that out or you'll get us both kicked out of here."

"You said you'd sort it," I say.

"I did. Sort it."

I sit back, folding my arms. "You know I didn't mean it like that."

"Do you fight with every guy who takes you for a steak dinner?" He grins like he knows no guy has ever taken me for a steak dinner.

The waitress returns with our drinks, but Darragh waits for my answer.

"Only the ones who trick me into it," I answer lamely.

"So you get tricked into a lot of dinners? I'm not surprised." He takes a deep swallow from the glass.

"What does that mean?" I ask, not touching mine. A part of me wants to rebel a bit longer.

"You're very hostile and snappy. The only way to deal with you is to trick you."

"You're not nice either. You're very arrogant and mean." I drink my Coke as he digests my words.

"Mean?" One eyebrow arches in amusement.

"Yes. Mean," I say.

"Give me an example."

"I have examples coming out of my ears. You called me a dyke."

"You called me gay," he fires back.

"The moment we met, you thought I was a worker," I say with raised eyebrows.

"But you are a worker." He says each word slowly.

"I'm a cleaner."

He snorts. "A prostitute. Yeah, that was a stupid mistake." He laughs.

"See, you just did it again." I sit back, so done with talking to him. He just can't help himself.

"You're confusing the shit out of me. First, you're insulted that I think you're a pro, and now you're insulted because I don't think you're one. You have to make up your mind, blue."

"I'm not explaining myself," I answer as the waitress arrives with our food.

Darragh rubs his hands together and inhales deeply.

I can't stop the smile that spreads across my face.

When he notices I haven't started to eat, he looks at me. "Dig in."

I do and the food is divine.

"So what do you do other than pretend to be a cleaner?" I ask when my stomach starts to fill up.

"I'm a farmer," he says.

I choke on a chip.

Darragh has to smack me on the back until I cough it up. *Real ladylike.*

"You don't believe I'd shovel shit or pull the tit of a cow?" He grins.

I roll my eyes. Everything is about sex with him. "You like it?" I ask. Both his brows raise in surprise.

"I'm going to a party tonight. You want to come?"

Now I'm laughing. When I realize he isn't messing, I sober up and take a drink of Coke. "You're serious?"

He nods.

"Hmm. No," I answer.

"If you change your mind, text me," he says.

I look at him sideways. "Sure," I tell him.

I don't have his number to text him, and he doesn't have mine. He's just trying to be friendly. The food is like lead in my stomach, and I put my knife and fork down.

"Are you finished?" he asks, still eating.

I nod and sit back and take in the restaurant with its amazing artwork and chandeliers that sparkle over our heads. I wonder what it would be like to have money, to be able to have an operation like this. What would it be like to burn your friend's money because you could? To have steak for your lunch or get paid to sit on the floor and watch someone clean? Life is funny.

The extremes between Darragh and I are stark. I wonder if he's put here to remind me of how far I am from a life without financial worries. The divide between us is so large.

"You okay?" Darragh asks.

I sit up. "Yeah, just thinking about Peaches," I lie.

"That your girlfriend?" Darragh smirks.

I place my knife and fork neatly on my plate. "My cat. I'm not into girls."

"Okay, calm down." He wipes his mouth on the napkin and pulls one leg up onto the other as he faces me. Being this close to him is intimidating. He's a big guy, and this close you'd think you'd find a flaw, but I can't, not even a blemish. Sitting this close makes me more aware of myself.

I take the napkin and dab my mouth.

"So you have a *pussy* cat." He keeps a straight face.

"Are you that deprived of a woman's touch that you can't stop talking about sex?"

He snorts at my question. "You saw me yesterday."

I nod. "Yeah, with two women you paid to touch you."

"I don't always have to pay them, sweetheart. Just sometimes I like to take control."

I shake my head, telling myself to let it go. "No, I bet you've never really been intimate without being drunk or high."

"You're wrong again. I actually have."

I'm not buying what he's selling. But my face is on fire, so I need to get off this topic. "Have you got any pets?"

"Yeah, lots of them." He winks, and I'm not sure what he's implying.

The waitress makes her way to our table, stopping my response. "Was everything okay?"

She looks at me a bit longer before diverting her attention to Darragh. Is she wondering what a guy like him is doing with someone like me? I'm tempted to tell her I'm only here because his spoiled ass wouldn't sit in the canteen. If his brother hadn't threatened him, we wouldn't be speaking.

"Perfect, thanks," Darragh answers and hands her his gold card.

I gather my lunch and stand up as he waits for his card. I mumble a thank-you. I know I owe him, and I don't like owing people favors. We leave the restaurant and go back to the room we were cleaning. The moment we enter, Darragh sits back down in his spot. I don't know why, but I really thought he might actually help.

"What's your number?" he asks.

I glance at him, and he widens his eyes at me while holding his phone. I recite my number to him and jump a few seconds later when my phone vibrates in my apron. I take out my phone and see an unknown number fills the screen.

"It's me," Darragh says with humor. "Just thought you tricked me. That would be your style."

I'm not sure what to say. I save the number as Man Whore and slip the phone back into my pocket.

We finish the rest of the ten rooms and pack up to go at four o'clock. There's an awkward moment as I stuff things into my locker, because Darragh just stands there.

"I'll see you tomorrow," I say, wondering why he isn't leaving.

"You need a lift?"

Yes, I do. "No. I already have the taxi planning to come."

"You sure?" he quizzes and I nod.

"Okay, blue. See you tomorrow." Darragh's voice sounds cheerful. I'm left in the locker room, unsure how I'm feeling at all.

CHAPTER SEVEN

DARRAGH

"ARE YOU SERIOUS?" I scream at DJ over the beat of music. I can't believe he brought Mark here.

"Look, he's ready to forget the whole incident with you beating him. I swear I'll keep him in line."

Gripping DJ by the back of his neck, I pull his head close to mine. "You better," I warn him.

He grins. "So we good?"

I smirk. "Not even close."

His grin slips, and my smile widens.

The club is full and the music vibrates through the floor. The moment Art spots me, he's up and howling into the air like a fucking wolf. High as a kite, he jumps off the couch and hugs me.

"The king is here."

My eyes land on Fitz, who's wearing the same fucking clothes he wore when we robbed the ATM. I need to replace his money. The guy needs it badly. "What's up, Fitz?"

He smiles while bobbing his head and nursing a bottle of beer in his hands. No doubt the liquid is warm. I was late to the party.

Art throws his arm around my shoulder. "You need to take a piss?"

I pause, not sure why. But another part of me thinks fuck it, and I walk with him to the bathroom.

The drugs work quickly, and I can't seem to focus on myself in the bathroom mirror. Blood trickles from my nose, and I wipe it away before washing my hands in the sink. I spot a girl in a small silver dress as she walks into the men's toilets. Art finishes up, and he stares at her as she walks past him.

"Is that bad coke?" I ask.

He shakes his head. "Nah, that's good stuff."

The girl hikes her dress up and backs her ass into the urinal and pisses. Art pulls out his phone to take photos of her.

"You're a dirty bitch," I say.

She gives me the finger. "Was busting to go." She stands up and pulls her dress back down.

I remind myself not to touch her later. She winks and walks past me, and I shudder.

"That's fucked up," Art says, stuffing his phone into his pocket.

We reenter the club. Art disappears, showing the photo to anyone who will look at it. I stay with DJ, Fitz, and Mark, who wants to be my best friend now. That shit will never happen. I drink way too much, and my nose burns and bleeds from all the coke I snort. I'm sweating, so I pull off my jumper, but my body doesn't want to cool down. My heart feels like it's skipping a beat. I sit back and clutch my chest.

"Put your clothes back on," a gruff voice sounds from above me.

I open my eyes to a large guy all dressed in black standing over me. "Fuck off. This is VIP, and I paid a grand to have the section for the night."

"You have to put your clothes back on." The hulk isn't listening.

I pat my chest to find it bare. My trousers are on, but my socks and shoes are also gone.

"I'm too hot," I mumble and close my eyes. Hands grip my arm, and my eyes snap open. "Take your big, ugly hand off me," I say.

He ignores me and pulls me up from my seat. Glass shatters across the floor, and I stare at Fitz and the broken bottle in his hand. Laughter bubbles up my throat. The security man doesn't remove his hand from mine but calls for backup.

"Let him go now," Fitz warns.

The jackass doesn't listen. I push my body weight against his, and the move is unexpected. We tumble down the few steps that lead up to the VIP area. The crowd scatters. We fall and they start cheering for us.

The noise, the drugs, and the painful thump in my chest make me feel possessed. I lace into the security man. I'm no match for him, as he's fucking huge, but I get a few thumps in before I'm pulled off and dragged outside.

When the Gardaí arrive, I'm disappointed in the security. "Can't take care of me yourself?" I sneer as two Gardaí approach me. "You got to ring in reinforcements?"

"Gardaí Síochána. Have you no real criminals to catch? Always arresting the innocent citizens."

One of the Gardaí takes a statement from the security man. Fitz is dragged past me, laughing his head off. A second squad arrives, and he's put into the back. The cold of the night is starting to hit me, and I shiver.

"Gardaí," I call.

He looks at me.

"I'm freezing. Would you mind putting me in the car?" I ask.

The fucker ignores me.

"You're useless at your job. Out here breaking up bar fights. You must not be fit to catch the real criminals. How do you sleep at night? Your wives must find it hard to get aroused looking at you two messes."

One of the officers rams me against the wall. "You'd do well to shut your mouth, Darragh."

"Oh, you know my name. I'm fucking terrified."

"I said shut up."

The security man relays his terrifying tale of his assault to the Gardaí.

"You're a pussy," I say.

The other Gardaí comes and places me into the back of the car, banging my head in the process.

"I'd hit you back, only that would be animal abuse," I sneer.

The door slams in my face, and I sit back in the seat and close my eyes.

Two more doors slam, but I keep my eyes closed.

"You're in serious trouble," one of them says.

I want to tell him to fuck off, but the rumble of the engine puts me to sleep. Cold air rushes in as the door opens again. I'm dragged from the Gardaí car and into the station.

"Take it easy, you moron. My feet—" I tell them, but they move me faster.

"You think you're funny. You will be laughing when I find out where you live." He hits me on the back of the head.

"You think you're the big man with your baton?" I push myself against the Gardaí, and he hits me back, then he pushes me back and I stumble but catch my balance.

The other Gardaí, the one with the receding hairline, pushes me forward and doesn't stop nudging me until they close the door to my cell.

The bench is cold as I lie down and hug myself. I just want to sleep.

Blood. There's so much blood. I'm staring at it on my hands, and my eyes follow the trail that soaks up into the blonde hair. The girl's head is open, and maggots crawl everywhere.

My eyes snap open as I roll off the bench and empty the contents of my stomach onto the ground. The creek of the door opening doesn't stop the assault on my stomach.

"You've made bail."

The words are spoken with humor as I bring up bile before standing straight.

"I was starting to like this place," I say, wiping my mouth with my arm. "Enjoy cleaning that up." The Gardaí's irritation makes my vomit on the floor almost seem sweet.

"Get out." His hand digs into my back as he pushes in front of him. I'm tempted to turn around and push him back.

A guy in a suit stands with his back to me. It's Liam. I'm fucked now. Liam is signing something while they remove the handcuffs from my wrists. He doesn't turn around to make sure I'm following him. We make our way to his Range Rover. He opens the door, and I climb in and shiver again as he starts the Jeep.

"I'm starting to think they're targeting me," I say, stealing a quick glance at Liam.

He doesn't react.

"Look, man, I know it's shit, you having to bail me out. But I didn't do anything wrong this time." I sound pathetic.

No response.

"Liam."

"Yes, Darragh?" Liam is focused on the road. His voice doesn't rise or fall. Nothing.

Clenching my fists, I face the window. "Nothing."

Silence fills the Jeep and seems to stretch out like the dark road in front of us. All want is a smoke, but I don't have them on me.

***

We pull into the garage, and it's then that Liam speaks. "It wasn't me. He took the call to come down and get you."

"Father?" I ask, staring out the window and into the dark space.

"We meet him in the library."

I glance at Liam. I want him to tell me it will be okay, but he gets out of the Jeep.

I shiver again as my bare feet touch the concrete floor. The smell of rust from the recent rain lingers in the air.

"Get some clothes on. I'll meet you at the library." Liam doesn't linger, and I follow behind him, taking the stairs two at a time.

When I open my bedroom door, I want to collapse on my bed. It's unmade and I move toward it. Rubbing my face, I start to look for socks, shoes, and a clean shirt. After getting a fresh pack of smokes and a lighter from my stash, I light one up as I walk through the house. I need it before I face these two.

Both of them sit across from each other, each in a suit. At this hour in the fucking morning? It has to be six, six thirty maybe.

"Put out the cigarette." Father doesn't look up at me as he speaks. I take two final pulls before putting it out in a large crystal ashtray that sits on a small round table near the couch. When I look up, it's Liam who's watching me. He points to another large couch across from him and Father. Nothing like an interrogation this early in the morning.

My ass is only just on the couch when Father starts. "I'm at a loss with you, Darragh. Each time I think you've settled down, you do something stupid." His voice rises on the last word.

"I'm sorry. It won't happen again." The lie comes easily.

"It will. It keeps happening." Father's calm voice makes me sit up straighter. I glance at Liam, who hasn't taken his eyes off me.

"I'm cutting you off." Father stands and places a hand into his pocket. He stares down at the rug as he speaks.

"What does that mean? From the family?" My heart starts to pound.

"No, Darragh."

Relief has me sitting back.

"From my money. You will have no access to any funds."

I grin, but it slips as my heart jackhammers in my chest. "How would I buy anything?" I ask through gritted teeth.

"Get a job," he snaps.

"I have one. Remember?" I bite out the last word.

Father gives me a warning look. "Sitting on the floor in each room that's being cleaned is not working. Unless you start working, Darragh, there is no more money."

"Fine. Take your money. I'll get my own," I say, standing.

Father steps into my space. "How, Darragh?"

"I'll work for Liam." I'll really just rob another ATM.

Father stares at me until I shrink a little. "I remember the day you and Finn were born." His voice hasn't softened, so I don't confuse this with a nice moment.

"You nearly cost me my wife that day. She lost so much blood."

I drop my eyes as guilt dips and swirls in my stomach.

"Are you fucking serious?" a familiar voice asks.

My head snaps up as Connor enters the study. He's holding boots and socks in one hand, and a T-shirt is slung across his shoulder.

"You're blaming a baby for Mum losing blood during childbirth?" Connor's laughter bounces off every wall.

"This is a family conversation," Father barks.

"No, this is you two bullying Darragh. Does it make you feel big, Liam?"

I want to be like Connor when I grow up. But he has nothing to lose. I have everything.

Liam stands up and takes a step toward Connor. "No, it makes me feel old. And you may feel your aggression here is justified, that you feel better standing up for Darragh, but you have no idea what goes on inside these walls."

Connor pulls his shirt off his shoulder and holds it. He takes a step toward Liam and I move. I'm not sure why or what I could do, but fear curls in the pit of my stomach.

"Exactly, Liam. All the secrets you two keep." He shoots a hateful look at Father. "You are as bad as him."

Connor looks at me. "You don't have to stay here and listen to them. You're a grown man. You can leave."

I swallow the emotion that rises. I do have to stay here. I wouldn't survive anywhere else. I know that. He knows that. So his false hope isn't welcome.

"Get out," I say to Connor.

His body goes slack with my answer.

"You heard him. Get out of our home." Father steps forward.

"That's not—" I try to explain myself.

"Shut up." Father is facing me now, his wrath growing, strangling me. I nod and I can't look up at Connor.

"I don't want you in my home anymore. You're not welcome," he shouts at Connor.

I stare into the fireplace like a coward.

Connor snorts. "I can't stand you wankers anyway." His gaze meets mine, and the hurt is there. I want to say I'm sorry, but he turns his back on me and leaves.

"I don't want him here again," Father tells Liam.

Liam nods.

My stomach tightens. "You won't hurt him?"

Both of them look at me. I don't know if it's the drink or the idea of having more guilt on my conscious, but I need to know. "Liam," I beg.

"What is wrong with you?" Father asks. "Are you on drugs?"

The tightness in my stomach travels up and closes around my chest. I need to calm down, but something in me is clawing, fighting to get out. "Answer me." I face Liam. "Will you hurt him?"

"Sit down, Darragh," Father barks at me, but I can't calm down. I can't stop looking at Liam. He won't answer me.

"Just tell me you won't hurt him. Please." I step even closer to Liam, but Father steps in front of me.

His face is red from my disobedience. "I said sit down." His final warning.

If I let this go, I won't get an answer, and no answer feels worse than Father's wrath.

I glance at Liam. "Please, Liam," I plead to the brother I know still lives inside this sociopath.

It all happens so quickly. I know the moment Father is going to hit me. He moves toward me quickly, and I brace myself for the slap that never comes.

"Don't," Liam warns him. It's one word, but it's like someone just flipped the Monopoly board. Father stands back, his fists still clenched, but he doesn't touch me.

"I won't hurt Connor," Liam finally says.

I'm not fucking sure what to make of all this. The flip in power. Father obeying Liam. I stare at Liam, not really sure what I'm looking at. A new fear creeps up on me, and I shrug as if the movement will make it go away.

"You're at work in three hours. You need to shower and get dressed."

I nod and step away from Liam. I don't look back at my father as I leave the study and return to my room.

The smoke curls around me as I lie on my bed and blow it toward the ceiling. I try to make sense of what just happened. Father listened to Liam—no, he obeyed him, like Liam was running the show. Maybe power had shifted and they weren't telling anyone.

Shane wouldn't like it. Something deep down tells me it wasn't that at all.

CHAPTER EIGHT

CIARA

When I arrive at the first room, Darragh is waiting at the door. There's something different about him this morning. He's staring at his shoes. When my trolley wheels squeak, announcing my arrival, he looks up at me. He smiles, but it doesn't reach his blue eyes.

"Morning," I say and open the door. He steps in and sits on the floor. Once I have my trolley in, I move to open the curtains.

"Could you leave them closed a little while longer?" he asks, and there's something in his voice that has me agreeing. It's a tenderness I've never heard before. I start to clean the room, stripping the bed while stealing glances at Darragh. His sullen mood is a side of him I haven't witnessed yet.

"I often wonder what it would be like if my mum was still here." Darragh speaks softly, and I don't want to stop cleaning, so I get my duster and polish off the trolley.

"She nearly died when I was born." He's staring at the floor, and it's like this knowledge is eating him away.

"What happened?" I quiz and half polish the bedside tables.

"I'm a twin and she had to have a C-section. Dad said she nearly bled to death." He's frowning.

"Did she?"

Darragh's head snaps up, and he's looking at me like I just slapped him. "No, not then."

So she's dead.

"What happened to her?"

His clenched fists and quick rise and fall of his chest have me wanting to withdraw my question.

I leave him in his own turmoil and polish the TV and dresser.

"She was murdered." His words are harsh.

All the hairs rise on my body, and my hand stills on the dresser.

"I still picture her gasping for air. Her nails were painted red. Like a blood red. She always kept herself so well."

"I'm sorry," I say.

He shrugs and forces a shaky grin.

"You were there?" I ask.

He tilts his head, narrowing his eyes. He looks more alert. "No, I wasn't..." He sounds so defensive.

"It's just what you said about her gasping for air..."

"Sorry. She was shot, but I wasn't there. I had a mental night last night. My head's still all over the place. I got myself arrested." He stands now.

"You sound proud," I retort.

Darragh stares at me and it's uncomfortable. I relax when he turns away and opens the curtains, letting light stream in.

"What about you?" he asks.

I put the polish and duster away. "What about me?" I fire back.

Darragh opens a window, getting ready to light a fag.

"You can't smoke in here," I say.

He lets out a heavy breath before putting the fag back into the box. "Aren't you the rule enforcer?" he says with a grin.

"No. I just can't afford to lose my job." I grab my gloves and supplies for the bathroom. What I don't expect is for Darragh to follow me in. He takes a pair of gloves from the box and blows into them before he slips them on.

"What are you doing?" I ask.

"What can I do?"

"You want to help?" I'm surprised. His six-foot frame in the bathroom is making the space seem small. I want him out.

"My father has cut me off from the family money, so I need to work to get money." That's all it takes and I relax. "I was thinking that maybe you were doing it because sitting on the ground while I do all the work just might be getting to you. But obviously I was wrong." My words come out harsher than I intended.

"Don't sound so pissed, blue. I mean, I want to help you too."

I roll my eyes and turn my back on him. "Clean the sink," I say and then think maybe I should make him clean the toilet. Fingers coil around my arm, and my reaction is immediate.

"Take your hands off me." I rip my arm from his and square up.

Darragh holds his hands in the air. "Wow, wow, calm down."

I'm trying to control my pounding heart and tell my body he's not a threat.

"You'd be really pretty if you let your hair down." Darragh's words have me blinking.

"You're hitting on me?" My confusion works itself around my words.

"No. If I was hitting on you, you'd know about it."

"I suppose, then, ignorance is bliss," I say, but my mind is scrambling.

"Why do you take everything as an insult?" he questions.

I hate the way Darragh's making me feel. My brain is scrambled, and my mind is in chaos. I don't like it. "Because, Darragh, it usually is."

I don't miss the soft knock on the door, so I quickly evacuate the bathroom.

"Ciara." Liam's eyes scan the room. Everywhere his eyes touch, he gives a nod of approval. "I need you to come down to the club. We're getting ready for tonight's opening."

I nod. "What about my rooms?"

Darragh steps out of the bathroom.

"Darragh will finish them," Liam informs me.

I don't turn to Darragh, and he doesn't respond.

"Are you ready?" Liam isn't leaving without me.

That feels odd. I check my apron for my phone and key. "Yeah, I'm good to go." I follow Liam out of the room, and when I turn to say goodbye to Darragh, he's disappeared back into the bathroom.

***

The new part of the hotel is alive with activity. The room is nearly complete, and the last touches are being placed. A man carrying a large flower arrangement walks past me. I snort. This is going to be a strip joint. I'm not sure any punters will be looking at the flowers. Some dancers are practicing, fully clothed, but that isn't stopping the males from ogling them as they work.

I line up with the rest of the staff when Liam arrives back out. "Uniforms are ready in the changing room, so everyone should get ready and we'll start your training."

Everyone moves.

"Ciara." I hate being singled out, especially by Liam. "Your uniform size needs to be adjusted."

"I'm an eight," I tell him.

He nods. "I'll have a uniform ready for you shortly."

Great, can't wait.

Another man carrying a larger vase of flowers walks past me, and I see Liam's retreating back. I'm not sure what to do, so I just start wiping down the tables while I wait for someone to step in and tell me what I need to do. It doesn't take long before Sharon, one of the managers, comes looking for me.

"Ciara." She beckons me over with one finger. Her nails are stupidly long, but she doesn't exactly work. Delegating is definitely her specialty.

Sharon flicks her long red hair across her shoulder. "Get changed. Your uniform is in the changing room." Sharon steps away. "Derek, move the flowers. They're obscuring the bar."

I leave and find my uniform on the bench in front of my locker. I hold it up. It doesn't seem so bad. The black trousers are the same as for us cleaners. I hate how they stick to me, but they're comfortable. The red shirt is tight, and I have no choice but to unbutton the first three buttons. My chest is too large for the shirt. I leave and fold my arms across my chest as I try to find Sharon. She's still out on the floor giving orders.

"My shirt's too small," I inform her, dropping my arms so she can see for herself.

She looks me and up and down and grins. "It's perfect."

"It's not, Sharon. I feel very exposed."

She leans into me. "You'll get more tips." She turns to everyone else now. "Okay, ladies, listen up."

All the other girls have changed, and everyone's uniform looks pretty tight. No one else seems uncomfortable, but I am.

I refold my arms across my chest as I fall into line with the other girls. We spend the next hour learning how to carry a tray with one hand. A lot of glasses get broken, but toward the end of the hour, we all seem to have it. So that's what we will be here for, to serve.

"Looking good, ladies." A familiar voice rings out across the room.

I nearly drop my tray but balance it at the last minute. Darragh strolls in with a smirk on his face and a fag tucked behind his ear. His confidence fills each step he takes. He winks and grins, and when our eyes meet, his widen and he takes two steps toward me.

"I knew it." The way he says it has my face burning.

I'm praying to God that he doesn't say anything inappropriate. "I knew you were hiding this"—he points to my chest—"under all those layers."

I glance at the other girls, who look at me like I just materialized. "Did you clean all your rooms?" I fire back, hating how he's so easily embarrassing me.

"I'm on my lunch break." I thought my words would deter him from poking at me but not a bit. "Thought we might grab some food."

He's talking to my chest, and I wish I didn't have to hold the tray so I could fold my arms.

"Darragh." Sharon arrives back over and puckers her lips. Darragh's attention is taken off me, and now he focuses on Sharon. She embraces him and plants a kiss on his cheek. I hate how my stomach twists at the sight of her lips on him.

"Sharon, you look hot," he tells her, and she smiles at him.

I stop myself from rolling my eyes, knowing some of the girls still watch me.

"Aren't you a sweetheart," she says. "Did I hear you mention lunch?" She bats her eyelids, and I feel disappointed when Darragh agrees to go for lunch with her. I know I shouldn't—it's Darragh and we don't exactly know each other, but yeah, that hurts.

"Ciara, are you coming?"

I'm placing the tray on the table when Darragh asks me. I turn, flickering a glance at Sharon, who curls her lips up in distaste.

"I'm good," I say. I can't meet his eye.

"Come on. Don't make me drag you." He's in front of me now, and everyone is staring at us.

My heart starts to pound. "I brought my lunch."

He grins. "Bring it with you. I'll sort it."

I can't stop the grin that spreads across my face. "Like you did the last time?"

His own grin turns into a smile. "I promise I will sort it this time."

I don't believe him.

"Ciara is training, so she won't be ready for lunch for a while." Sharon smiles, but it's forced and she's looking very jealous.

"You want me to have a word with the boss?"

It's like Darragh knows he's winding Sharon up, and I wonder for the first time if I'm a pawn in his game. Is he trying to make her jealous? The burn of my chest has me turning away.

"I have work to do." I walk off with the burn of humiliation heavy on my cheeks.

It takes a full ten minutes before the heat leaves my face and chest.

"A word please, Ciara." Liam's voice comes from behind me.

When I turn, he walks off to the bar and I follow him. I can't think of any reason Liam is pulling me aside, unless it's to talk about working later, or maybe Darragh didn't finish the rooms, which would make sense.

"Can I get you a drink?"

The question surprises me. "Like a Coke?" I quiz.

"A Coke," he calls to the barman.

I don't want a Coke, but I don't refuse it as Liam places it on a mat and slides the mat toward me. He waits and I take a sip. He seems satisfied once I put the glass back down.

"Have you wondered why I paired you with Darragh?"

An uneasy feeling starts in my stomach. "No." I had wondered, every day since he was placed in my room.

"I selected you. It wasn't random. You, Ciara, are different from other girls." He lets that sink in.

I'm not entirely sure what he means. "Thanks," I say, but it sounds more like a question.

"Darragh has a weakness for pretty girls. He likes to break them. So with you, I knew it would work."

I grip the glass, hating what he's saying, but I'm not naïve in thinking I'm a model. But Jesus, he's making me feel like a monster. He's silent now, and the burn of my throat has me wanting to leave. "Is that all?"

He runs his long fingers across the polished bar. "Earlier, he asked you for food. I saw your face. I just don't want you to be naïve about the situation."

I pick up the Coke and drink nearly all the contents. "I'm not naïve. Don't forget where you found me," I say and stand up.

A nod of his head is my dismissal. I'm hurt, but at least with Liam, he's straight. No mind games.

The day he offered me a job and climbed into a brand-new Range Rover, I remember staring at the Jeep thinking I could be walking to my doom. He hadn't leaned out of the vehicle, but his voice reached me. "Are you coming or not?"

I walked to the car door. “I won’t work the streets,” I told him with a hand on my hip.

“It’s a cleaning job.”

“How can I trust you?”

“You can’t.” His honesty had me taking my chances and climbing into the Jeep.

***

I eat lunch alone in the canteen. The other girls had tried to be friends with me when I first started. I’m not a people person, and now with Darragh, I’m starting to really hate humanity.

CHAPTER NINE

DARRAGH

I WASH SHARON OFF me before heading to Kells to meet the lads. She isn't my type, but she's more than willing to relieve some of my stress, so I let her. And she also paid for my food.

A win-win.

"Did you miss me?" I ask as I enter the warehouse. I'm not sure of the reception I'll receive; everyone is here. It's DJ that comes over to me, and for a moment, we stand toe to toe. He raises his hand, and I clasp my hand with his.

"We good?" he asks, already grinning, knowing we are.

"Yeah, we're good." He releases me and takes my phone out of his back pocket and places it in my hand.

"Nice one," I say.

He also hands me my wallet. Not one card will work, since Liam canceled them all. That's why I need to get this next job done.

"Everyone ready for tonight?" I ask as I take a seat beside everyone else. Art hands me a drink and I refuse. I don't want this job to go wrong. I want to have my mind focused. Everyone looks at me like I'm a fucking leper.

"I want a clear head," I tell them, but I don't look at Mark. His presence here is good. It means I didn't piss him off enough for him to go to the Gardaí.

"There's only one thing," DJ says.

I nod. I don't want them to know how desperate I am.

"You burn our money this time and show's over, man."

I grin and shrug like I'm pretending to consider it. "Let's make sure no one pisses me off, then."

DJ turns away from me, not happy with my reply. Art snorts a laugh. He doesn't give a shit. Money is plentiful to him.

"So everyone knows what they're doing?" I ask this while looking at Fitz. He's in the same white hoodie with the hood pulled up.

"You know I am," he says, fixing the legs of his tracksuit bottoms.

"Am I with DJ again?" Mark asks.

I look to DJ. It's his call.

"Yeah, you're with me," DJ tells him.

Art snorts one line after another. "I'm with you, man," he says to me, while inhaling quickly through his nose.

I itch to join him, but I don't. Everything will be the same as the last time, only this time we're hitting Kingscourt. It's very close to home, but the layout is similar to Kells—a single street. It makes it easier to block.

Art robbed a Range Rover. The shiny black surface reflects my face as I climb in.

"You couldn't have gotten something a little more inconspicuous?" I ask.

He jumps into the passenger seat with ease and starts going through the CDs like he knows what he 's looking for. "It's my Dad's." His grin spreads wide across his face.

"Have you fucking lost it?"

"He deserved it. My Dad's an asshole." He peeks at me with a smirk before returning to the CDs.

I know he doesn't have the best relationship with his dad, but stealing his Jeep?

We wait until everyone else has left before we leave the warehouse. Art blares the music while he pretends to play drums on the dashboard.

I want to feel the high he's feeling. I hate how slick my hands are right now or how I'm thinking of all the things that could go wrong. I normally don't give a fuck. Being sober might not have been the wisest. Art takes out a small bag of powder and snorts another line up his nose.

"You want some?" he asks.

I fold. "Fuck it, yeah."

I snort the line off his hand before sitting back in my seat and letting the drug flow through my veins. The feeling of panic disappears rapidly, and I turn up the music. The tightening around my throat goes slowly, and it's replaced with the sense of invisibility. We roar toward Kingscourt as I push my foot down harder on the pedal.

***

Hot air blows out of my nose, and my face feels itchy from the balaclava. It's restricting but I'll get over it.

Everyone is ready the moment I stop the Range Rover. Art gets out and climbs up on the digger. The gun is cold in my hands as I climb out and focus on the empty street around us. Music still blares from the Jeep, making my pulse pump and pound.

Art tears the ATM from the wall and puts it on the flatbed trailer in seconds. I give DJ a wave to leave, and he starts his Jeep. Art is running toward me. I take one final look before climbing back into the Jeep.

Sirens blare and I freeze for a moment, my frantic mind wondering how the fuck we're going to get out of this. I unfreeze and race to the Jeep before jumping in and starting it. My foot pushes down on the accelerator, and smoke rises as the tires tear from the road.

Art grips his door and slams it as I take off, but the squad car in front of me blocks our way.

"Put on your belt," I say.

I clip mine in and tear toward the squad. The impact when we hit the front of it has our bodies slamming forward, but I don't stop. I don't lift my foot and zoom past them.

Art whoops and shouts as he glances out the window.

"They're following us," he shouts.

I can't stop the smile that crosses my face. "Let's put your daddy's car to the test," I say and he laughs. The Jeep roars onto Carraickmacross road. All the bends slow us down, and the Gardaí are able to keep up with us.

"You need to go faster, man," Art tells me as he snorts more coke up his nose.

"Can you hold off for five fucking seconds?" I rub my face as I look at the three squad cars who tear after us down the road.

When the bends disappear, it's only then I put distance between us and them. I can't push the Jeep any harder. The smaller Gardaí cars fall further behind, and I relax enough to pull off my balaclava. I turn down a back road. I don't slow down but keep pushing the Jeep. The roads aren't gentle to us, and we bounce around.

"Slow down before you snap my neck." Art's words have me slowing down. The night is quiet, and no sirens can be heard. I pull the Jeep into a field.

Art is out getting petrol from the boot. We douse the Jeep before lighting it up and take off on foot.

"Ring Fitz," Art says. "He'll come and get us."

I don't. Instead, I ring DJ. "You okay?" I ask, but really, I want to know if my money is okay.

"That was too close for comfort. What about you guys?"

"Yeah, we're good. What happened?" They got there too quickly. Like maybe they knew.

"Fitz rang me. The cops were chasing him, and he had forgotten to drop the spikes to slow them down."

Dumb fuck. "Where is he now?" I ask.

DJ doesn't answer, and an uneasy feeling skitters across my back. "I keep ringing him but no answer."

"Can you pick me and Art up? We're close to Dun na Ri Park," I say.

"Give me twenty minutes."

I hang up, and Art is staring at me. "Fitz fucked up. Forgot to drop the spikes."

"I'll beat the shit out of him," Art responds. His foot strikes the ground forcefully.

"He's not picking up his phone." I light up a smoke.

"You think he snitched?" When Art asks, I already know the answer.

"Nah, I just hope he didn't get caught."

***

DJ picks us up. The moment we're in the car, I know something is wrong. My first thought is Mark.

"Where's Mark?" I ask.

DJ starts the car. "Mark is at the warehouse, but Fitz was arrested."

"Fuck!" Art roars.

"Calm down, Art," I say and he sits back.

"What do we do?" DJ sounds nervous.

"I'm thinking," I tell him. "Just head back to the warehouse."

Mark is counting the money when we walk in. He pauses and looks at the three of us.

"I hope you're not pocketing any of that," I spit out before making my way to the fridge.

"Fuck you." His reply comforts me. I don't really give a shit if he does. I just need to figure out how to get Fitz out of jail.

"How much did we get this time?" Art asks, popping open a bottle.

I'm listening.

"If we split it equally?" Mark asks.

I stare at Mark before nodding.

"Ten k each." He grins.

"Scraps." That wouldn't last me long. Sitting down, I run both hands across my face before picking up my bottle and drinking half of it. I really only have one option.

I take my phone out and ring the one person who can fix this.

"Darragh." Liam's voice makes me reconsider.

"How's it going?" I ask. Everyone is watching me, so I get up and walk away.

"Are you in trouble?"

I hate how he already knows I'm not ringing for a chat. "Of course not. Can't one brother ring another?"

"I'm working, so can we continue this social conversation at home?"

"Fine. I need your help," I say.

Silence fills the line, but he hasn't hung up, so that's good.

"A mate got arrested for speeding. Could you send—"

"No. Is that all?"

"Liam, I'd owe you," I say.

"I said no."

What an asshole.

"Fine." I hang up and turn to everyone, knowing they're waiting to hear if I can fix this.

"Sorry, guys. He's temperamental these days."

Art's phone dings. "He's been admitted to Navan Hospital," Art says, looking back up. "He flipped the car. Minor injuries."

"Who told you?" DJ asks.

"Cathy, one of the nurses. I texted her and asked her about Fitz."

"Are you sleeping with her?" DJ asks really slowly.

"Of course he is." I shake my head as I grab another drink.

"She has a banging body. Not a great face, though. But it's good to have someone for information like this."

"Well, nothing we can do now, only celebrate," I say.

No one has fully relaxed. I grab a drink for DJ and Mark, and we stand together in a circle.

"A bit of a fuckup, but it could be worse," I say, and we click our bottles together before we all take a long drink.

That night, we do a lot of drugs, until bliss is everywhere.

"I love you," I tell Art as I light a fag.

"I love you too, man."

"I mean it. You're like my fucking rock. I know you got my back," I say while throwing my arm across his shoulders.

"Don't burn me." He moves away from my lit smoke, so I move it to the other hand.

"You could always buy a new jumper," I tell him.

Art grins. "But I like this one."

"You know my family is filled with pricks." I inhale again and watch the smoke fill the space above my head.

Art widens his eyes like he's trying to stay awake, before slipping away from me.

"Great talk," I mutter as I get another bottle of beer.

Sitting back on the chair, I watch as Mark and DJ hobble around to music that blares from the radio that's propped up on the wall. Both of them are stoned out of their heads. Art continues to snort too much coke up his nose, and sitting here in this shed reminds me of the fucking losers they are.

I down the rest of the bottle and leave it sitting on the ground as I get up and leave the warehouse. No one notices me as I slip out and into my car.

***

I check myself in the bathroom mirror in the hospital. My eyes are too wide. Cold water splashes my face, and I meet my eyes again in the mirror. I check my pockets for more coke; just a little bit more would settle me, but I come up empty. I must have already taken the last of it.

It's seven in the morning, and the hospital is quiet as I seek out Fitz. He's in the male ward, finally out of that fucking hoodie. The blue gown makes him appear sickly. The bruises across his face are stark, and one leg is wrapped up in a cast. The nurse's station is lit up. I can make out three of them drinking coffee and chatting, but no one is on the ward. I move quietly over to Fitz and shake him until he wakes up.

"What's up, bud?" I greet him.

His eyes flicker around the room, and fear is visible on his face.

"What did you tell them?" I ask.

"Nothing, I swear. I'm loyal to you, Darragh." His mumbling is waking one of the guys beside us.

"Shh. That's not what I asked. What did you say to them?"

"I was drinking and driving when the Gardaí followed me. I panicked and drove away. That's it."

"Excuse me." One of the nurses, who's carrying more weight than what's considered a good advertisement for the health service, shuffles toward me.

I stand to my full height and raise both eyebrows while my lips lift slightly in a smile. "Good morning, nurse."

"You can't be in here." Her cheeks tinge red as she gets closer, but she's holding firm to the hospital's policy.

"Just visiting a friend," I tell her. Fitz, the stupid fucker, doesn't back me up.

The nurse finally looks to Fitz, who nods like a dummy.

"I was just leaving." I turn to do just that, but she's on my heels.

"I'll walk you out."

"No need," I tell her, but she's still following me. "I suppose the walk would do you good," I fire over my shoulder and her face flames.

"Excuse me."

I walk faster, but she manages to keep on my heels. She's like a dog with a fucking bone.

"Look," I start, "I know you don't often get to walk this close to someone who looks like me, but you can fuck off now. I don't need a chaperone."

Her face slackens, and her washed-out eyes hold mine steadily—something I didn't expect from her.

"Security." She marches over to the reception desk. "Marcella, get me security."

I'm still walking away from her.

"Don't move, sir."

I pause. "Or what? You'll eat me?"

She shakes her head in disgust, and I turn just as 'security' enters the building. The guy in front of me can't be more than four foot six, with a bald head, decaying teeth, and a frame that threatens to fold if I touch it.

"What's the problem, Mary?" He's removing a walkie-talkie from the strap on his black trousers.

Mary, the heifer, is moving toward us. "I caught him in the male ward, and when I tried to escort him out, he became hostile and abusive."

"I was visiting a friend," I tell the security man, who's still staring at Mary. "I wasn't abusive."

"Backup to the front of the hospital," he says into his walkie-talkie. "We have an abusive man on site."

"What the fuck?" I need more drink to deal with this shit. I try to sidestep the sideshow, but the security man blocks me. I could pick him up and move him aside, but as three more enter the building, all ready for action, I decide to take a deep breath.

"What's the problem?" security man number two asks Mary.

"Have you no work to do?" I ask Mary. She's really getting on my nerves.

"Don't speak to her, sir." Security man number three, who is a similar height to my six foot, steps forward. The handlebar mustache makes it hard to take him seriously.

"I'm leaving. No harm done." When no one moves, I try to rein in my irritation. "What the fuck do you want?" I take a step toward the security man. "Money? An apology? Blood?"

"Calm down, sir," the short man says, with his hand looped into the belt of his trousers.

I try to step around them again, but I'm blocked. The third guy is out with his walkie-talkie. I can't hear what he's saying into it.

"Have you been drinking?"

"You're hospital security, not the fucking Gardaí. I see what's happening here. You all went and sat the entrance exam to become a Gardaí and failed, so this is the best you got. And fat fucking Mary here, tries to make herself feel better by helping the sick while her own sickness"—I turn to Mary—"which we know is eating, is out of fucking control."

"How dare you." Mary's wide eyes start to water.

Sweat is gathering on the back of my neck. I need a hit before I snap. I move, and when they block me this time, I push forward. The short one hits the ground, like someone throws a game in a football match. The other two shuffle in front of me with arms outstretched. They keep moving backward but don't touch me.

Once we get outside, they seem to sigh as the Gardaí pull up and two of them make their way toward me. I'm so fucked today.

CHAPTER TEN

CIARA

THE NEW CLUB IS filled with punters, but the room is kept cool from all the overhead fans. The low lights and sultry music make me want to leave and have a shower. I didn't think I would ever crave to be back cleaning toilets, but this place is making my skin crawl.

Women with bodies to die for wrap themselves around poles as the music changes to a more upbeat tempo, some singer telling them to *work, bitch*. Men lounge everywhere, their eyes wide with lust as they sit back sipping drinks and enjoying the show.

The table I serve seats two men who ooze money. The blond-haired guy has a split down the center, his hair falling to his ears. I can't keep up with the amount of times he runs his hands through his highlighted hair and flashes his pearly whites around the room.

"Two martinis," I say with a smile as I place them in front of Blondie and his mate, who didn't get picked in the looks department. His black hair is gelled back, A false tan and overwhitened teeth make his overall appearance too much.

A wink from Blondie is sent my way. At first, I straighten and check behind me. His deep laugh has me staring back at him, my eyes immediately flashing to his teeth.

"What's your name, sweetheart?" he asks.

I hold the tray loosely between my fingers and keep the smile on my face. "Ciara. Is there anything else I can get you gentlemen?"

It's like watching a peacock showcase his colored feathers. The word gentlemen seems to have that effect on Blondie, as he puckers his chest out further. His friend gives me a dismissive wave, his eyes staying trained on the pole dancers.

"Your number?"

Blondie isn't my type, but I'm pretty sure I'm not his either. That's why this conversation isn't making sense. "I'm sorry. We aren't allowed to mingle with clients. Is that all, gentlemen?"

Blondie isn't giving up. "Tell me your boss's name, and I'm sure I can sort this out."

"No, thank you." I don't wait for this conversation to get anymore awkward. I leave, but the sting to my backside has me standing up straighter. When I turn, I expect to see Blondie, but it's his friend.

"Get to work," he says while he sits back.

My chest tightens, and sweat has gathered between my shoulder blades.

"What are you looking at?" His question is taunting.

"Leave her alone." Blondie comes to my defense, but he looks uncomfortable as he runs his hands through his hair.

I move before I hit him with the tray. I'm waiting for someone to say something to me as I move back through the room. In my head, I think everyone just witnessed what happened. But as I move around the growing crowd, people are in their own conversations, smiles on their faces and alcohol filling their mouths.

Once I reach the bar, I grip the counter. I focus on the cold wood as I move my fingers in the direction where the carvings along the edge take me.

My heart falls back into a normal rhythm, and I release the tray and place it onto the bar before running my hand across the top of my head and down my ponytail. I need to pull my shit together. Looking up, I keep my eye on my table and wait for the nod that I dread.

"This place is crazy." Sinead moves beside me. Her blonde hair is up in a high ponytail, but unlike mine, hers sways perfectly. The shine of her hair reflects the light. Lips smeared in pink lipstick grin at me. "It's such fun, isn't it?" she asks me.

I force a smile. "Yeah, it's great."

Simon, the barman, moves down to us. "What do you ladies need?"

"Vodka with a dash of Coke and a beer," she orders and he moves away to get her order. I take a peek back at my table. Blondie meets my eye and nods.

"You want to swap tables?" I ask Sinead sweetly, but her own smile falls.

Her eyes narrow. "We have to stay at our assigned tables."

"I don't remember hearing that."

"Well, I do." She snaps her head, her ponytail moving quickly as she faces forward.

The crowd seems to grow closer as I hold the tray to my chest and make my way to my table.

"Two martinis?" I say with a smile to make this as quick as possible.

"Yeah, thanks, Ciara." Blondie still smiles at me.

"No. I want..." His friend takes up the drinks menu and really assesses it as Blondie smiles up at me.

I glance at the female dancer, who wraps her body easily around a pole.

"You could be like her." Blondie says it like it's a compliment.

"I'm good."

"What's this?" The asshole that touched me has his head buried in the menu. His eyes rise and meet mine, and I have to walk over to him and lean in way too close to see what he's pointing at.

"A slow screw against the wall," I say.

His lips tug up on one side, and it's creepy as fuck.

"I'll take one of those." His eyes are on my breasts as he speaks.

My breaths come in quick spouts, and my chest strains further against my shirt. I turn quickly, and the sting to my backside is like the crack of a whip. I'm moving but not toward the safety of the bar; I'm moving to him. My fist connects with his nose, and I know I've broken it. Not by his roars or the gush of blood that sprays from his nose, but by the crack. I'm smiling in victory, but it lasts for only a moment as people around us shift back.

"You broke my fucking nose."

My head snaps back to him, his eyes ablaze with fury, but I don't feel fear. I wouldn't mind round two. The pole dancer in front of us is barely moving, as her attention, and most of the room's, is on us. Security moves in from all sides.

Blondie hands his friend napkins, but they're whipped out of his hand. "I want her fucking arrested for assault."

"What happened?" Security asks, and I let the asshole scream that I broke his nose.

"He touched me," I say in my defense. I don't expect them to drop it, but I do expect them to remove him.

Instead, the second security man takes my arm. "This way."

I resist as he tries to move me without any commotion. "What about the pervert who touched me?"

The security man looks up at the guy in question. Justice would be served.

"I never touched her. She's a liar and obviously a liability to this establishment. Who's going to cover my medical expenses and my pain and suffering?"

"Your pain and suffering? I've been serving your creepy ass for the last hour. What about my suffering? Less time on the sun beds, and I'm sure that will cover the cost to your nose. It was crooked anyway." I'm nearly spitting as the security man drags me away, like I'm the criminal in all this. It's not until I'm in the hall and the music is distant that I think of my job. I can't lose it.

"Where are you taking me?" The concrete floors and sterile white walls have my stomach twisting.

Neither security man answers me. My arm doesn't come loose from their steel grip as I yank it back.

"Stop it," one warns as we turn into a room with just a table and chairs.

"What is this?" It looks like an interrogation room from a movie.

"Stay here."

I don't have a choice as the door slams behind me. I try it immediately, and it doesn't open. The room is missing that huge two-way mirror. It's not that no one is watching me; a small camera in the corner is recording my movements. The chair is hard as I sit down and put my head in my hands. I really made a mess of this.

The door opens and the security man who was first on the scene comes in. His face is still as stern as he stands on the opposite side of the table. He inspects me and I do the same to him. He's tall like all the rest, maybe a little over six feet, with broad shoulders and a wide face. His hair is cut close to his head, leaving only the shaving of hair. Green eyes observe me without blinking. There's nothing significant about him; he's average. He doesn't wear the arrogance like a lot of bouncers I know.

"He touched me," I confess, gripping both hands together.

"You don't work in this part of the hotel. What were you doing there?"

"Okay, I see you're not very bright. What, you think I was serving drinks to assholes for the fun of it?"

His grin is immediate, but he suppresses it quickly. "We don't have you on the staff list."

I shrug. "That's not my fault."

He exhales loudly. "We need to get confirmation that you were assigned to work there."

I fold my arms across my chest. "Fine, but I better be getting paid while sitting in here."

His eyes flash with humor. "You broke that guy's nose."

"He's lucky that's all I broke." My bravery is slipping. The thought of getting fired over this is scaring me, but I hold his eye.

"I'll be back shortly," he says.

I don't speak as he leaves but focus on my nails. They never grow. I've tried the nail polish that strengthens them and is supposed to be some miracle grow formula, but no, my nails always remain short. Fake nails aren't something I can wear in my line of work. Still, I would at least like them a bit longer so they look more feminine.

The door opens and my stomach squeezes. My heart beats faster as Liam steps into the room. He frightens me. It's his unemotional state. Even now, everything is precise as he closes the door gently behind him and moves to the table.

He carefully pulls out the other chair and sits down so we're very close and eye to eye. I swallow and the small bit of bravery I felt shatters across the concrete floor.

"I'm sorry."

"For what?" Liam always takes each movement in. I haven't been in his company much, but when I am, I often feel like he observes others reactions and movements, like he's learning. It's unsettling.

"For causing a scene." I don't say for breaking the guy's nose, because I'm not sorry.

The way he holds my gaze causes my chest to rise and fall quickly again. The strain on my buttons has me trying to calm my heart. Liam doesn't look down at my chest; his focus is on my face.

"Life is cruel, unkind, and most often, our decisions are based on what life shapes us to be. So you strike out at a customer for touching you. In one sense, it's justified." He pauses before continuing. "But can you imagine if everyone acted on their instincts, acting with brutality? What kind of place would this be?"

Heat rushes to my cheeks. It's how I survived on the streets. Well, at the start not so much, but I learned fast. It was a kill or be killed kind of world.

"He touched me," I repeat, but my words fall flat. I'm going to get fired.

"He won't be in this establishment again."

Surprise flitters through me. "But what about his nose?" I ask stupidly, and then kick myself. I need to shut up.

"It will heal." Liam rises and places the chair gently back in its place.

I don't know what I'm waiting for—the other shoe to drop, maybe. This all seems to have gone so well.

"Ciara." My name has me looking at Liam. "You've been warned now. The next time you act without thinking, your time with us will be up." And the other shoe falls.

I nod.

"If that happens again, you report it to security and the person will be removed."

I swallow the emotion that rises inside me.

"You can go back to work," he finally says.

I'm standing on shaky legs. When I leave the room, I don't return to the floor. Instead, I go to my locker. I just need a minute. The water feels nice on my burning throat. Liam is fair, but his words seem to swim deep and take root inside me.

Every unwanted touch, every slap rushes me. I take out my phone and search for a distraction and am surprised to see a missed call from an 049 number, which is local. I ring it back just to distract myself.

"Navan Gardaí, how can I help you?"

"Hi. I have a missed call from this number."

"What's your name?" The Gardaí asks, sounding half-distracted.

"Ciara Michaels." I chew my lip as I hold the line. I have no idea what this is about. But after breaking someone's nose, it's looking like the creep has reported me. My stomach twists. What would happen if someone filed assault charges? I could end up with a criminal record. A fine.

A familiar voice fills the line then. "Ciara, you gem. I need your help."

It takes a moment for my fizzled mind to catch up. "Darragh?"

"Yeah, so I'm in a bit of a situation. I got arrested last night and need you to bail me out."

"Why me?" I ask, utterly confused.

"You're my friend."

I snort. "You're such a liar. Anyway, I can't. I'm in trouble here and can't leave."

"Why, what happened?" His concern sounds genuine.

"I broke some guy's nose."

He's laughing. "Did you get fired?"

"No, but I need to get back to work," I say.

"Hold on. Seriously, I need you to bail me out."

I chew the inside of my mouth. "I'm finished in a few hours. I can do it then."

"I can't survive another few hours."

I close my locker door, aware of the amount of time I'm wasting. "Darragh, it's a few hours or nothing. Which is it?"

He lets out a heavy breath that holds no humor. It's filled with exhaustion. "I'll let you know."

Guilt gnaws at my stomach as I finish the bottle of water and make my way back onto the floor. A few people give me looks, but I serve my new table while ignoring them. The men smile at me, so the news that I was violent hasn't spread yet. It's an easy shift, but my mind is stuck on stupid Darragh and his pitiful voice. I know what sitting in a cell feels like. I know what it feels like to not have anyone come sign you out. The Gardaí usually just got sick of me and let me go.

I make a stupid decision as I ask Sinead to take over my table.

"We already talked about this." Her voice fills with bitchiness.

"They tip really well and it's all yours."

"Even the tips you've made already?"

I force a smile. "Yeah."

"Fine, but you owe me."

I don't have a clue how she figured that one out, but I nod and get off the floor. I'm questioning my motives in what I'm about to do. I can only assume that fresh wounds have come to the surface for me today, and I hope I'm thinking straight as I knock on Liam's door.

"Come in." His voice gives me pause.

After turning the knob, I step in. "I was wondering if you have a moment."

He points at the chair in front of him. The door closes behind me, telling me there's no going back. The chair is comfortable and I sink into it, but under the circumstances, I don't want to get comfortable, so I sit forward.

"I got a call from Darragh. He's at Navan Gardaí station and needs someone to bail him out."

"And he rang you?" His eyebrows rise slightly.

"I'm as surprised as you," I say.

"Thank you for letting me know."

I'm getting up, but I pause behind the chair. "So... are you going to get him?"

"Does my brother's welfare concern you?"

"No," I answer too quickly. "I was just curious."

Liam stares at me, and I shift uncomfortably.

"Okay." I'm not getting an answer. I leave the office and feel no further along.

Now, a different kind of guilt churns in my stomach. I feel like I've dumped Darragh into a mess. He hadn't rang Liam, and maybe there's a reason for that.

CHAPTER ELEVEN

CIARA

I'M BACK ON THE floor, and the work is a great distraction. The club is alive, and no one looks at me strangely. I'm serving tables and time flies.

After a while, I get that feeling like someone is watching me. When I look up, it's Blondie, who's sipping a beer at the bar. I raise a brow at him, and he raises his drink. He's alone at the bar, but I feel uneasy with him here. I continue serving drinks and try to ignore his eyes, which seem to burn into the back of my neck. Three security men are close to me, and my shoulders loosen. I just need to be aware of where they are.

Sharon moves around the room. She offers nods to servers who are doing a good job and raised eyebrows to any servers who aren't moving quickly enough. When my customers leave, I tidy up their table.

"You can keep the bar area clean and check the floor for any rubbish," Sharon says as she scans the room again before she meets my eye.

"Of course," I say.

When she leaves, I do as she asks, and the closer I get to Blondie, the more irritation claws up my back. I hate being watched. I pick up some glasses and move right beside him as I wait for Simon to come and take them from me.

"What do you want?" I ask, not looking at him.

"Your number?"

Now I look at him. "No. Not because I'm not allowed, but because I don't like you." I say it quickly as Simon arrives and takes the empty glasses from me. "Leave me alone or I'll hurt you," I warn him.

His easy smile is gone, and the saying 'birds of a feather flock together' comes to mind. But I don't wait around for a response. I'm back on the floor, weaving through bodies as the beat has the dancers wrapping themselves tighter around the poles and the men moving a little closer to the stages.

When my shift finally ends, I just want to wash it all off me. I want to go back to cleaning rooms. This isn't going to work well for me. I just know it.

I check my phone—no messages from Darragh. I consider ringing Navan Gardaí station to see if he was bailed out, but I remind myself that this is none of my business.

I grab my bag and leave work.

Outside, I inhale the fresh air. The sound of the music still beats away in my ear. I need to ring a taxi. My car is still broken, so I need to get it fixed as soon as possible. Taxis in Kingscourt aren't readily available. I ring the one number I have, and it goes straight to voicemail.

"Great." I walk away from the hotel and out the front gates. Cars come and go, but one slows down beside me. I keep walking, but I'm aware of it.

"I was trying to be nice to you." Dread curls in my stomach at Blondie's words.

I hold my phone tightly in my hand. "If you don't go away, I'm ringing the Gardaí," I threaten, but his car still rolls beside me. My pace quickens, and he easily finds a stride beside me.

"Come on, get in. I'll give you a lift."

"My lift is on the way," I say, considering walking back to the hotel. But it's bright and lots of cars are coming and going. I don't think he's going to hurt me. He's just trying to intimidate me.

"I know you're lying." His words hold a smile.

I stop walking and face him. He stalls the car. When I look inside, I see the other guy. "What do you want?" I ask.

"You broke my nose, bitch. You can't get away with that."

I laugh at him as his face reddens. "What are you going to do?"

Blondie is out first, and I try to hold my stance.

"Make you pay." His nose is bandaged, and bruises blossom under each eye. There's no blood on his shirt, as he wears a fresh white one.

"Get back into your car before I hurt you again." My threat doesn't sound so great now as they move closer. Cars whiz past and that's what's keeping me calm. It's daylight. They won't hurt me while the world watches, but something has me moving away. Sharp stone bites into my back, the hotel boundaries stopping me from moving any further.

Blondie is the first to touch me. His fingers wrap around my arm. I quickly pull it free and start dialing 911 on my phone. The screen cracks as it hits the ground.

"You're not ringing anyone, *Ciara*." The way he says my name has me thinking he's more dangerous than his friend, who's moved around the car and is closing in on me.

"You want money? I can get you money," I say.

"Do we look like we need money?" Blondie opens his arms and points at his car. It's new and flashy.

"Everyone always wants more," I say, my eyes snapping to my broken phone.

The other guy reaches me, and I move back out of his way, causing the stones to bite into me painfully.

"Look, you two freaks. Fuck off now before I start screaming." My voice rises.

The cars that move past us are going at high speed, the noise drowning me out. Their grins tell me they know no one will hear me. I dash to the left. Fingers grip my hair, painfully whipping me back.

My reaction is immediate. I start swinging, and my fist connects with Blondie's jaw the same time the other guy takes a swing at me. I can't avoid it, and the impact is worse than I remember. It's been a while since I've taken a hit. My ears ring and my heart slams painfully against my rib cage. It's like waiting for a gun to fire, and when it does, it either makes you freeze or move. My fist collides with him over and over again, until I'm dragged backward.

"Stay the fuck down," Blondie tells me before his foot connects with my stomach.

I gasp for air as he walks away from me and picks up his friend while dragging him to the car. Loose pebbles burn into my palms as I push myself off the ground.

The air is still thin as I try to catch my breath. My broken phone is beside me. I pick it up along with some loose stones and fire them at the car. Glass shatters and Blondie ducks for cover.

I don't stop but keep picking up whatever is accessible to me. I'm down to just pebbles, but I continue to fire them at his car. Small scrapes and dents are visible, and it feels like victory, that is until security comes running down the hill and out the front gates of the hotel. My first reaction is relief, until they reach me.

Hysterical girlish screams tear from Blondie's mouth. "She jumped us and beat up my friend."

"They attacked me first. They waited for me outside." I'm touching my face, which seems to ache even more now. My hands tremble. Shock is starting to settle in.

"She vandalized my car," Blondie roars as he holds his phone to his ear.

"Everyone needs to calm down." The security man holds out a hand toward each of us.

I'm calm as I gather my bag off the ground. The ringtone is loud as Blondie rings the Gardaí. While he's occupied, I get my phone off his front seat. I'm surprised when it switches on. The screen is cracked, but it still works. The other security man moves around the car. Moans erupt from behind the car as Blondie's friend starts to sit up. Cars slow down, catching glimpses of the commotion.

It doesn't take long for the Gardaí to arrive. The moment they do, Blondie is on them like a fly on shit.

"You need to arrest her…" He's pointing an accusing finger at me.

I stand hunkered, clutching my bag, hoping the whole 'little ole me' part comes across and that the Gardaí don't arrest me.

"Calm down and give us a moment." They approach the security men first to see if they saw anything.

I'm asked next. "You want to tell me what happened?"

Blondie throws a wobbler. "She attacked us," he roars.

"You need to calm down."

I can't hide the small smile of victory I feel as the Gardaí speaks to Blondie.

"Look at my car."

"Sir, last time. If you don't stop, we will take you all down to the station."

My smile is gone now. "You can take his statement first," I say quickly, just wanting this to end.

"She broke my nose." The other guy moves around the car, his face a mess. Blood drips from a cut on his lip. I don't remember getting his mouth. I was just hitting out blindly.

"I'm taking her statement first." The Gardaí gives everyone a final look, and when no one says any more, he turns to me.

"I work in the hotel." I keep my voice low, quivering. It's not that I'm lying, but I need him to believe me. "I was serving these two gentlemen, and when I turned down an advance, this one slapped me on the behind." I point to the asshole who did it. "I ignored it and continued working until he did it again. The second time, he hurt me."

"She's a fucking liar. She was coming on to me."

"Okay, arrest them all." The Gardaí pockets his small notepad.

My heart slams heavily against my chest. "No, I didn't do anything."

The two men are handcuffed and placed into the back of the car. The click of the cuffs on my wrists is familiar. I hate it.

"You can't put me in the back with them," I protest, my soft voice gone.

The Gardaí ignores me and makes me bend my head as I'm placed into the back of the squad car.

We don't speak as we're driven to Navan Gardaí station. The heat in the car has carved a path down my spine.

"I don't understand why I'm being arrested." I lean forward as I speak to the Gardaí.

"Assaulting people. Destroying their property," Blondie barks beside me.

If my hands weren't cuffed, I'd elbow him in the face. The Gardaí don't answer me, and I sit back.

***

Thankfully, we're separated once we enter the station. The room I'm taken to is small. The Gardaí that arrested me is the one who removes my cuffs and sits down with a clipboard. I rub my wrists, mostly out of something to do. They aren't really sore, but the bonds aren't normal.

As the Gardaí looks at his clipboard, I observe him. He has day's-old stubble on his face, some hairs a soft gray coloring. He's only in his forties, but the gray doesn't look bad on him. Blue eyes flicker to mine.

"Your full name?"

"Ciara Marie Michaels," I say clearly.

He writes my name down, but I don't like his furrowed brows. His eyes snap up to me, and he looks at me differently now. "We spoke on the phone today."

That's why his voice was so familiar. I couldn't pinpoint it earlier. "Did we?" I ask with a smile and tilt my head.

"Yes, we did. Darragh O'Reagan rang you to bail him out."

I sit back in my chair, my pretend smile gone. "Look, I barely know him. I work for his brother..." Something tells me I'm digging a huge hole for myself.

The Gardaí sits up straighter with interest. "Which brother?"

"Liam O'Reagan. I thought I was being questioned about what happened today."

"I ask the questions, not you. So what exactly do you do for Liam O'Reagan?" The Gardaí sits forward in his chair. There's eagerness in his stance.

"I'm a cleaner. I clean hotel rooms," I say slowly, and I get a sense of comfort when the Gardaí deflates.

His eyes scan the form in front of him. "How do you know Darragh?"

I want to ask if this is necessary, but I answer his question instead. "He works with me."

A look of disbelief stretches across his face. "Darragh O'Reagan cleans hotel rooms?"

I don't know these people, but even I know how doubtful this all looks. "It's the truth."

"Okay, you want to tell me what happened?"

Finally. I tell him exactly what happened from start to finish, but as I get to the fighting outside, it all starts to sound sketchy. Like how I managed to fight off two men. Knock one out and wreck a car. I'm small, so I can see in his eyes it isn't adding up.

"That's the truth," I finish up with.

"Just like Darragh O'Reagan cleans hotel rooms." His eyes narrow slightly.

I want to say something smart, but I fold my arms across my chest and look away. This is all starting to look and sound pointless.

The Gardaí leaves and I try not to stare at the two-way mirror behind me. I hate the idea that someone is watching me. I wait for fifteen minutes, and when no one returns, I can't sit still any longer. My mind won't allow me to pause on what will happen if they don't believe me.

I face the mirror. The left side of my face is swollen and my shirt, which was already revealing enough, is missing three buttons. Great. I look like a slapper. I untie my blue hair, which is falling out of its bobbin, and retie it again.

Walking closer to the mirror, I stare at myself. Blue eyes nearly the same blue as my hair stare back at me. Cupping my face with my hands, I try to look through, but it's not possible. I sit back down and wait. I'm not sure how much time passes when the door finally opens. This time, two Gardaí step in. Both of them sit down, not speaking.

"I'm Gardaí Bernard Brady." This new Gardaí gives me half a smile, while the one who had questioned me focuses on the stupid clipboard.

"Can I go now?" I fold my arms across my chest, trying to cover myself.

"We just have a few more questions."

I let out a heavy exhale. "I'm tired and injured. I'm the victim in all of this."

My words cause Gardaí Brady to grin. "They look far worse than you."

"That doesn't mean I'm not the victim." I'm not fucking smiling.

His grin disappears quickly. "You said the car approached you outside the hotel grounds?"

I nod.

"You need to speak."

"Yes, that is correct," I say slowly.

"What were you doing walking along the road?"

"My car is broken, so I rang a taxi."

"Who swung first?"

"Blondie," I say.

"He swung at you first?" The question is said slower now.

"No, he pulled my hair, and I swung," I answer.

"So you swung first."

"In self-defense." I'm looking from one to the other, trying to make sense of this.

"Ciara, just answer our questions. When you smashed the car, where were the men?"

"Behind it." I say it low in hopes it goes unnoticed.

"So they weren't threatening you then?"

I'm shaking my head. They're twisting my words.

"Just answer the question, Miss Michaels."

"No, they were cowering behind it," I answer.

"See, this isn't looking so good for you." Clipboard guy finally looks up.

"Why's that?"

"Their stories match. Both claim you attacked them, and then they hid behind the car that you continued to smash up."

I'm rolling my eyes now. "They're full of shit."

He nods and stares down at the clipboard.

Gardaí Brady takes over. "You're looking at an assault charge."

My pulse flickers in my neck, and the air grows thin. The silence in the room isn't helping. Both of them watch me.

"But..." Gardaí Brady starts. Hope blossoms and it feels cruel. "If you help us with something, this can all go away."

"Help you with what?"

"Liam O'Reagan. We believe not everything he does is above board. So if you give us some information, this will be reduced to a minor assault, and then it will disappear."

Running the brothel isn't above board, but I'm not going to be the one to reveal that to the Gardaí.

"He uses really cheap soap in his hotel rooms..."

Gardaí Brady sits up sharply. "This isn't a game."

"No, it's not. It's my life. I clean hotel rooms. That's it. I don't know what you want me to tell you. I get a pay slip, lunch breaks, and everything is normal."

They're both getting up, and my heart hammers against my rib cage. I want to scream for them to come back, but I try to sit still as they leave the room. The breath that leaves me is shaky. What have I gotten myself into? I should have just gone right back to the hotel.

It takes them another hour before they return, and I'm feeling like a caged animal at this stage.

"You get to make a phone call to get someone to bail you out."

I'm staring at Gardaí Brady. Someone has to bail me out? This is a clusterfuck. I have no one to ring. My eyes burn. "I need my phone."

"You can use the station's."

"What, does the station have all my contacts?" I ask.

Gardaí Brady narrows his eyes, and he opens the door further. "This way."

I follow him down a small hall before coming out to the front desk. He gets my phone out of an evidence bag. I scroll through it as my mouth waters. I have no one to ring. My heart is fluttering in my chest as my eyes continue to burn.

"Problem?" the Gardaí asks, and it sounds smug.

"Nope." I pick up their receiver and dial quickly before I change my mind.

"Hi, I'm at Navan station and need you to come get me."

His laugh is deep. "You're joking."

I take a quick glance at Gardaí Brady, who watches me closely. "No. I wouldn't ring you if I had another option."

"Ah, so I ring you to bail me out, and you didn't come and get me. Instead, you told Liam, and now you want me to come and get you?"

It isn't worth groveling for. They can't keep me here forever.

"Fine. Forget about it," I bark and slam the phone down. I look at Gardaí Brady. "You need to return me to the room. No one is coming for me."

With a raised eyebrow, he takes me by the elbow and leads me back to the room.

"What am I being charged with?" I ask.

"Aggravated battery."

"What does that mean?"

"You could be looking at jail time." He moves to close the door, but I can't be left here with my thoughts.

"How long?"

"Anything from three to 264 days." He closes the door, my sentence still undecided.

I sit down and try to wrap my head around this. Instead, the tears come and they don't stop. I'm still crying when the door opens a while later.

"You've made bail."

CHAPTER TWELVE

DARRAGH

"We hear you're working in a hotel."

I'm signing my name to get Ciara out. After she slammed the phone down on me, I couldn't just leave her. Liam is going to be pissed that I skipped out on work, but fuck it. I can't just leave her here.

"Yep." I hand him back his pen. Tom takes it, but I hold it firm and his grin slips. "I hear your daughter's fit." I release the pen, and he doesn't stumble back like I'd hoped he would.

"Don't make me arrest you." His warning means fuck all.

I give a quick laugh that has his nostrils flaring.

"Stay here." He moves around the desk to get Ciara. It's nice being the one bailing someone out. It's always me being bailed out. The sound of footsteps has me turning back around as Tom arrives back with a very upset Ciara.

The left side of her face is swollen, her clothes are dirty, and her shirt is missing a decent number of buttons. The puffy red eyes have me looking at Tom.

"What did you do?" I'm taking a step toward him. Ciara crying doesn't seem possible.

"We arrested her for aggravated battery." His bullshit words have me looking at Ciara, who gathers her belongings.

"Are you okay?" I focus on her.

She looks at me, and I'm glad when she holds my stare. She nods.

"You'll get a notice in a few days for your court date for sentencing," Tom informs Ciara, and he sounds so fucking smug.

I'm ready to hit him as I watch Ciara tighten and stiffen.

"We'll see about that," I say before wrapping an arm around her. She lets me and that seems even worse. Every other time I've touched her, she's reacted badly.

"Look, don't worry about it. We'll sort itout," I say while opening the car door for her.

Once she's in, I look back at the station. Three of the Gardaí are out front, staring at us. I hate how they smile, like they have somehow discovered my weakness. I won't let Ciara pay for my crimes. I give them a grin and the finger before getting into my Audi and tearing out of Navan. I can see the dust in the mirror.

"You've got to say something, Ciara." I light up a fag as I hold the steering wheel with my legs.

"Thanks for bailing me out."

I take a quick look at her as I take the steering wheel back in my hands. She's staring out the window.

"You want to tell me what happened?" Rolling down the window, I blow out the smoke.

"It wasn't my fault."

When I look at her this time, she's staring at me. Her blue eyes are no longer sparkling, like they had been back in the station. Now, they burn with anger, and that makes my shoulders relax.

"They waited for me outside the hotel. I was walking along the road..."

"Wait, why were you walking on the road?"

Ciara shifts and faces me more. When I glance at her, all I see is boobs. Her shirt has really taken a beating.

"My car broke down, so I rang a taxi."

"You should have rung me," I say, but once the words leave my mouth, I know how stupid they sound.

"What, you're running a taxi service as well as a cleaning one?"

I don't answer her as I inhale deeply and blow smoke around the car instead of out the window.

She clears her throat. "Anyway, they cornered me. Blondie pulled my hair, and they were going to hurt me, so I reacted."

I'm grinning. I shouldn't be, but I wish I'd been there to see it. "Look, let's get the footage from the hotel."

"They have cameras outside the grounds?" Hope fills her words.

"Yeah, I'm heading that way anyway, so may as well kill two birds with one stone. I was working and Liam's been ringing nonstop."

We're close to the hotel now. After throwing the fag out, I roll up the window and take another peek at Ciara.

"We need to get you a shirt, Ciara."

At my words, she clutches her chest.

Pulling into the parking lot has me feeling slightly apprehensive. Liam won't be happy.

"You shouldn't have left work." Ciara speaks when I turn the car off.

"What, and leave you in a cell?"

Her cheeks turn red. "I'm sorry I left you."

Taking out the keys, I unbuckle my belt. "I know you couldn't leave."

Ciara stares back at the hotel, and as I study her side profile, I can see how scared she really is.

"We'll fix this," I say, and her attention comes back to me. Her eyes roam my face, and it's odd but I shift under her full stare.

"Why are you doing this?" she questions. Her eyes flicker from my lips up to my eyes. "I won't sleep with you," she fires out before I can answer.

"Talk about shooting a guy down." I grin at her. "You're my friend."

She shakes her head and looks away. "Be serious, Darragh."

I touch her shoulder gently, and she looks at my fingers, which I remove before she finally looks at me. "I am serious. You don't owe me anything. I just want to help."

"Why?"

"Why can't you just say thank you?" I can't understand why she's resisting help.

"Because nothing comes for free. Everything has a price tag."

"Ciara, if you don't want my help, fine. But I'm just trying to be the good guy here." I open my door and hope she gets out too. When she does, the relief is immediate.

"Come on."

She keeps her arms crossed over her chest as we walk into the hotel.

***

We're in Liam's office watching the footage from outside the hotel. Liam wasn't happy when we entered his office, but he's obviously willing to help Ciara since we're watching these two scumbags follow and corner her. Watching her being manhandled has me looking at Liam.

"Do you have their names?" I ask him, and he doesn't answer me with words. We watch to the end, and once Liam switches it off, I sit back down.

"I will forward the footage on to the police. They will drop the charges once they see it was self-defense. And you should go home." Liam stands.

I try to protest, but he raises a hand a warning to me that I heed. Liam picks up his phone and orders a taxi for Ciara. I want to protest again—I can drop her home—but I keep my mouth shut.

"If you need some time off, Ciara, that can be arranged."

"No, thank you. I'll be back to work tomorrow. I really appreciate you sending on the footage."

Liam nods and Ciara stands up.

"Thanks for everything." Her words are directed at me, but I hate how Liam is watching me, so I just give her a nod of my head. When

I can't resist any more, I look at her. She's staring at me, and her eyes shine with hurt. Her lids flutter down, cutting me off, and she leaves Liam's office.

"Why her?" Liam asks as he removes the footage from the recorder and places it into a plastic cover.

"What?"

"You left work to bail her out. Why?"

"She's a girl, Liam."

Liam shakes his head. "Who's broken beyond repair. No good will come from that Darragh. Leave her alone."

"I bailed her out. I didn't propose to her. Relax." My neck itches with a fresh coating of sweat. Ciara is broken, but so am I. I'm not going to sleep with her. I just want to help her.

"You're lying. Maybe you're lying to yourself. You need distance from her. I'll assign you to someone else."

I stand because this is Liam's controlling bullshit. It isn't about Ciara.

"No. I'm working with Ciara, Liam. I'm not working with anyone else. Me and her have a system," I say.

"I know. You sit and watch her clean."

I'm staring at Liam. "There are cameras in the rooms?" Of course there are. It's Liam.

"You never know who will be using our services. You can go back to work now."

I'm dismissed.

"I stay with Ciara." My words don't sound as strong.

Liam agrees. "For now."

I head outside for a fag and ring Connor. He's been churning around in my head, and when he doesn't answer my call, I don't blame him. I sold him out. We hurt each other all the time, but no matter what, we have to forgive each other. But isn't that the O'Reagan way? No matter what, we have to forgive one another and stick together.

I don't put the phone back in my pocket but send a message to Connor, hoping it will break the silence. **I have a job if you're in.**

***

When I arrive to work the next day, Ciara is already there, pulling a bed apart like it did something to her. "What did the bed do?"

She startles, turning quickly. "Darragh, you can't creep up on me like that." Her anger dissolves by the time she reaches the end of the sentence.

"I work here too."

She continues stripping the bed. I take a pair of blue rubber gloves from her tray and blow into them before slipping my hands inside. They barely cover my hands. The pillow I pick up has a white case over it, which I yank off and toss onto the pile Ciara made on the floor. I know she's watching me, wanting to ask me what I'm doing, but I continue removing pillowcases.

"That wasn't so bad," I say with a grin.

She laughs. "Now we have to remake it, polish, vacuum, check the wardrobe, and refill the tea and coffee before we move on to the bathroom, and then it's the next room. When that's done, all the rubbish and laundry have to be sorted. So let's see by the end of the day if it's that bad."

"Has anyone told you that you're very cynical?"

"No, you're the first," she says it with a straight face.

Ciara takes out fresh sheets and spreads them out. They wave across the space, and I grab my side. When the sheet settles, she's looking at me, smiling, and my heart gives a thump.

"What?" I ask.

"You're being very helpful lately. First you bail me out of jail, and then you get Liam to help me, and now this." She tucks the sheet down along the side.

"So you owe me," I say, balling up the sheet and stuffing it with all my force under the mattress.

Ciara sees what I'm doing and moves around to me. She pulls it out and shakes her head. "I'd hate to see your room." As she speaks, our shoulders brush.

"Is this reverse psychology because you want to see my room?"

She's laughing again. "I told you. I'm not sleeping with you."

"Yeah, so you keep saying." I'm not grinning now. She keeps saying it like it will never happen. "My brother is getting married in a week."

She shoos me out of her way so she can fix the other corner of the bed before she grabs the duvet.

"Which one?" she asks.

"Liam," I answer. The disbelief on her face has me smiling. "I'm messing with you. It's my brother Finn. We're twins."

"Liam getting married just doesn't seem possible. Can you imagine the pictures?" she says.

"Leave him alone. He just has a resting bitch face."

She's smiling again as she puts on the duvet cover. I let her work at that one alone. I don't want to have a used duvet that close to my face.

"Anyway, I need a date. So are you free?"

"Nope. Sorry." Her answer is immediate, and she doesn't even flinch.

This is so fucking strange. "You don't even know what day it is."

She throws a pillow at me, which I catch. The force behind it tells me she isn't as unaffected as she wants me to believe.

I take a step toward her, and her lids flutter closed. "I don't like weddings."

"Me neither. But I need a date. I can't go on my own."

"I don't own a dress." She's bending.

"I can sort it," I say.

She shakes her head, tightening the pillow to her chest. "I can't dance."

"Me neither." I take another step toward her. I don't know what the fuck I'm doing, but she's getting flustered and I like it.

"Let me think about it."

I pick up a pillowcase and give a quick nod. "By the end of the day," I say.

She agrees.

We finish the bedroom in silence, and once we start into the bathroom, I'm not feeling as hopeful about her coming.

She's scrubbing the toilet with her back to me. "If I do say yes, I'll need a bag and shoes."

"So it's a yes."

She glances at me over her shoulder, and my smile has her standing straight. She's still clutching the toilet brush, pointing it at me.

"Put the weapon down," I say, holding my hands up.

She points it toward the ground. "I'll go. But I swear, Darragh, this is a favor. I'm not sleeping with you." Her conviction is stitched into each word.

"Why would you think I would sleep with you?" I cross my arms over my chest.

Her cheeks redden. "I don't. But I'm just saying."

"Why are you so adamant on it? I'm curious."

"I saw you with those girls, and Sharon talks. It just seems that you would 'do' anything."

Her words are light, but I fucking hate them. "Don't worry, Ciara. I won't do you." The hurt that flashes across her face has me stepping towards her. "If you don't want me to," I quickly add.

Her face flames, and she turns her back to me and starts scrubbing the toilet again.

"So you're coming." I need to confirm that I haven't fucked it up.

"Yes. I'm a size eight. Shoe size five. Don't get me anything too revealing."

"Noted."

My phone dings and I slip it out of my pocket.

It's Connor. **What do you need?**

You're the best, Connor. I need to scare someone. You free tonight? I shoot back.

His response is quick. **Yeah, I'll pick you up at the house at midnight?**

See you then.

CHAPTER THIRTEEN

DARRAGH

It's freezing outside. I walk down the driveway, keeping close to the bushes with my bat in hand. Looking back at the house, I hope I'm not as visible as I feel.

I take out my phone and my heart deflates. It's twelve fifteen. He's not coming. The day back in the library has me understanding why he isn't coming. I stood there while they told him never to come near the house again.

Car lights shine in the distance, and when Connor's car pulls in, I'm jogging over to the passenger door and getting in.

"Thanks for coming," I say while placing my bat at the side of my leg.

"Beating someone up is what got me."

I smirk at Connor's response. "So are we good, man?" I gently punch his arm.

He reverses out onto the road. "Yeah. So where to?"

"Kells. We aren't really beating anyone up."

Connor slams on the breaks.

I hit the dashboard. "What the fuck?"

"Why aren't you wearing your belt?"

I rub my head as I sit back and clip in my belt.

"You said we were hurting someone."

"We're scaring someone. My friend DJ hit me and I owe him, so I thought two guys with bats showing up in his room would be a lesson."

Connor's stares at me for a moment before he sits forward and starts driving again.

"So you all set for Finn's wedding next week?" I ask.

"I can't wait."

I smirk. "Yeah, it seems everyone's holding their breath. Finn invited Auntie Trish."

"She's still alive?"

I'm laughing as get my smokes and lighter out of my pocket. "Yeah, I know. That bitch got nine lives."

"Who else is coming?" Connor asks as we move silently down the road.

I spark up the fag and inhale deeply. "All our relations. It's going to be one hell of a party."

Connor glances at me. "What, like even Michael's side?"

I roll down the window and blow the smoke out. "I'm pretty sure."

Connor focuses on the road, but his hands have tightened on the wheel.

"What's wrong?" My question has him loosening his hands.

"I just didn't think they spoke."

"Well, you know Finn. He's a goody two-shoes. He'll try to build bridges."

"Should be fun to watch them all burn down," Connor says.

I agree. Nothing good could come from this.

We roll up close to DJ's house, and I'm excited. I can't wait to see the little prick's face. We have our balaclavas on, and I pull Rochelle close to my side.

"He lives with his family, so we can't be too noisy. He sleeps downstairs. It won't be too hard to get in," I say as I tighten my hold on my bat and get out of the car.

We make our way around the back of the house, and I try DJ's window. It's locked. Connor takes over and pops the lock on the back door. We're in.

We step in on wooden floors, so we have to really watch our step as we make our way down the hall. The last bedroom on the left is DJ's. I can't wait to see his face. This will teach him not to touch me again.

Pushing open the door, I step in and Connor follows silently behind me. The room is empty. I glance around the room, the disappointment immediate.

We leave the house as quietly as we entered. I'll just have to reschedule for another night. I hate how pumped I am. Adrenaline still flows through me, no doubt through Connor too. We need to find something else to do.

Connor closes the back door soundlessly. I'm ready to leave, when low voices from the bottom of the garden have me smiling. I move toward the shed, and Connor follows me across the grass.

This is DJ's hangout spot away from his family. The closer we get, I start to recognize the voices. Fitz, Art, and Mark are here. Disappointment courses through me again. Tonight isn't our night. I can't do anything with everyone here.

"I'm not doing it, man. I'm not hanging him out to dry." Fitz's voice is close, and I move to the side of the shed. Connor is beside me. His eyes meet mine, but I focus on the conversation.

"He's the one that got us into this. If you don't sign the deal, we all go down."

"I can't do this either." DJ speaks up.

My heart stutters in my chest.

"I'm signing the deal." Art's words hold conviction. I know him. He'll sign whatever deal he's talking about.

"I thought you and Darragh were best friends." Fitz jumps to my defense.

At the mention of my name, Connor moves toward the shed. Gripping his arm, I shake my head. He doesn't come back, and my pulse spikes. If they see us, we can't stop what's happening.

"Fuck you, Fitz. I'm not going to prison for him. The bank jobs were his idea. So if they offer us immunity for him, I'm all in."

Fucking traitor.

I'm aware of Connor staring at me. No doubt the bank job part didn't go unheard.

"You can count me out." Fitz's voice floats away, as if he's moving.

I sink further into the shadows. Someone shuffles around.

"You can't leave, Fitz." Mark's voice has me clenching my fists.

"Leave him alone, Mark." DJ jumps to Fitz's defense.

"You're either with us or against us, Fitz. Or I'll make sure your name goes along with Darragh's." Art. I hadn't expected him to betray me. "Same for you, DJ. I have no problem dropping you in it."

"I'm not doing it." Fitz makes me proud.

"You really are retarded," Art sneers. "You're going to get raped daily in prison."

"Art, shut the fuck up." DJ's voice has risen.

Connor pulls on my arm. I know we've heard enough, but I'm waiting for Art to say he's made a mistake. That handing me over isn't an option.

"Are you in, DJ?"

"You know I'm in," Mark says.

"I need more time," DJ says.

"You fucking tell him, and you're a dead man." Art's threat has me clenching my fists again.

"Two weeks. That's all you have before we have to give our answer. If you don't do this, we all go down."

Connor pulls me again, and this time, I leave with him. Once we're in his car, I pull off the balaclava. I'm waiting for Connor to rip into me over the bank jobs, but he doesn't.

"You need to tell Liam." Connor clips in his seat belt.

I light a fag as Connor pulls out from the roadside. His suggestion has me looking at him.

"What? You know he's the one that will make this go away."

He's right. But I don't want 'this' to go away. He would have them all clipped.

"Darragh, this isn't a walk in the park. You're looking at ten plus years," Connor reminds me.

I inhale deeply while blowing smoke out the window. "Yeah, I know."

Connor pulls the car in on the hard shoulder, and I nearly hit the dash again.

"You need to listen to me." He's facing me now, and I'm listening. "They die or you die. Which is it?"

It sounds pathetic, but they're my only friends. "They die," I mumble while inhaling more smoke.

"You need to tell Liam." Connor grips my shoulder, enforcing each word.

Telling Liam would make it so definite. "I will. Just give me time." I glance at Connor, and he releases me.

He shakes his head. "No. You do it now."

"We have two weeks. Next week is Finn's wedding. We don't need this shit right now."

Connor slams his fist into the steering wheel. The horn rings loud across the open night. "You're the one behind the ATMs."

"Only two." I shrug, not sure what he wants. I don't regret it. If I could, I'd do it again.

"I wonder about you, Darragh. You don't need the money."

"Yeah, I do. They cut me off. I'm fucking cleaning rooms for my money." I reel my anger in. Connor isn't the target here. I'm not exactly sure who is. Liam, Father, or me.

"I'll take care of it, I promise. After the wedding, I'll tell Liam. Or in the meantime, I'll find a way to convince the guys not to sell me out."

Connor is shaking his head again, pissing me off. I throw the fag out the window and roll it up.

"They'll sell you out. Who else can they blame?" Connor starts the car and pulls back out onto the road.

I know he's right. If they don't hand me over, we all go down. I wouldn't fair too well in prison. "I'll tell him. I promise," I say again.

The house is dark when I get home. I go straight to my room and let the betrayal sink in. Out of everyone, I really thought Art would be the one who would have stood beside me. I got that so fucking wrong.

The bottom drawer of my bedside locker holds a half bottle of whiskey. I take it out and unscrew the cap. The burn is immediate, and I drink deeply. Telling Liam would get them clipped. I don't care about Mark, but Art dying doesn't sit right with me. Liam wouldn't let Fitz and DJ walk away either. I can't let them all die.

The whiskey sloshes in the bottle as I place it onto my bedside table before picking up my fags. After lighting a smoke, I lie back on my bed. The red tip glows in the dark room. Smoke billows over my head, and I try to just focus on it. But Art's betrayal is too fresh. I drink until I pass out on my bed.

"Oh my God. You need to clean this place up."

Opening one eye, I look up at Una. She's standing over me with her hands on her hips as she stares down at me.

"What are you doing in my room?" My head pounds as I speak.

Una moves out of my line of sight. Light burns my eyes. "Close the curtains." I bury my head in my pillow.

"You texted me last night." Una glances around my room, wriggling her nose. "This place reeks, Darragh."

"I texted you last night?" I'm sitting up even as my head and stomach protest.

"Yes, you did, asking me to go dress shopping with you. I didn't know you cross-dressed." She's smirking.

I'm struggling to function right now. "I need painkillers and coffee," I mumble through dry lips. I pick up the bottle of whiskey and drain the final three drops to try to moisten my lips.

"You know, you have a problem." Una's voice isn't playful this time.

I don't need a lecture. "Yeah, my head is banging." I get up, pulling the blankets aside.

"Oh my God!" Una's shouts don't help my head.

"What's wrong?" I ask, but she won't look at me. Her hand is covering her eyes.

Looking down at myself, I nod. "Ah, shit. I don't even remember changing."

"You're naked."

"Yeah, I know," I say, glancing at her back.

"Put some clothes on, Darragh."

I tug on a pair of jeans. "I'm decent," I tell her.

She turns around and her face is bright red.

"I think you like what you see," I tease and bend to pick up a T-shirt, but my head screams at me, and I stand again.

"You really need help."

"Get me a T-shirt?" I ask with one eye open. Una tuts but still rifles through my drawers and pulls out a clean blue T-shirt.

I throw it over my shoulder as we leave my room.

"So do you still want to go dress shopping today?" Una sounds cheerful now that we're out of my room and making our way downstairs.

"Yeah. It's for Ciara. I have to get her a dress and shoes and stuff for the wedding."

Una's squeal hurts my head. "You have a girlfriend. This is a first for you."

Mary is in the kitchen when we enter. "Morning, Mary," I say while pulling her into an unexpected hug.

"Oh, Darragh." Mary swats me away.

"What?" I ask, pulling on my T-shirt.

"You smell of drink. Sit down until I get you some food."

"Mary, I'm really considering marrying you," I say and she smiles.

"That would be unfair to your new girlfriend," Una sings as she sits down at the table.

"You have a girlfriend?" Both of Mary's eyebrows rise with surprise.

"No, just a friend who's a girl," I clarify as I sit down.

"So a girlfriend." Una is enjoying this too much.

Mary gives me two painkillers and a glass of water, which I take instantly.

"Tell me about Ciara." Una is bouncing beside me.

"Am I going to regret this?"

"Of course." Her laugh has me smiling. "Just describe her."

"She has blue hair. She can kick anyone's ass. She's hostile and violent."

Una frowns at my description. "She sounds like a keeper."

I laugh. "She's cool."

Una tilts her head. "If I didn't know you, Darragh, I'd say you liked her."

Mary has been listening, and she hands me a cup of coffee and some advice. "If she makes you smile, then she's worth it."

I take Mary's advice as I sip on my coffee. "I wouldn't say smile," I respond. "She amuses me."

"Okay, I need her body stats."

"She's five foot four, small build, big boobs." I grab my chest with my hands, and Una rolls her eyes. "She's a size eight in dresses and a five in shoes."

"Wow, what did you do measure her?"

"She told me her measurements, and that she wasn't coming unless I got her a dress and shoes."

Una laughs. "I can't wait to meet her."

"Meet who?" Shane enters the kitchen, and Mary immediately returns to the stove.

"Darragh has a girlfriend," Una tells him. I don't correct her.

Shane sits down beside Una, taking her hand like he still needs to make his mark on her.

"God help her." I ignore his words as Mary places a fry up in front of me. I give her a wink before I dig in.

"I'm going shopping with Darragh to buy her a dress." Una is spilling her guts to Shane. I don't interject but continue eating my fry.

"I don't know, Una," Shane starts.

I just want to eat my breakfast in peace. "Shane, go take your sister and entertain her yourself. I'll go shopping myself."

Shane's chair hits the floor, and he's over me.

"Shane, don't!" Una's standing too.

I continue to eat my fry.

"You're pushing me too far, Darragh."

I glance up at him. "What, you can insult me, but I can't tell you a truth?"

The air leaves me as my back collides with the floor. The chair screeches and stops as it hits the wall. Shane's over me, veins bulging. Una and Mary are frantic, and their noise has me closing my eyes. Sounds muffle and when it returns, so does the air and pain. My lungs refill and I choke.

"Shane."

I continue to cough as Liam's voice seems to dance across everyone else's, and silence falls on the girls. "Let him up."

Shane's still over me. I can see the struggle he's having letting this go, but I don't want to. I don't want to just let him be saved again by Liam. I don't want to be saved by Liam.

"Be a good boy and do as you're told." My words get the reaction I knew they would. His fist collides with my face. The pain races up into my already sore head.

Copper fills my mouth, and with the pain comes something else; it's a tide rising slowly, a rush, and I let it free. My own fist connects with his face, and the rush that I was deprived of last night at DJ's fills me. I get three good strikes in, and I know if I had Rochelle, I would make bits of Shane.

He's strong as we wrestle on the floor, knocking over chairs. Finn and Liam pull me off Shane. As I rise, he kicks out, connecting with my stomach, taking the air from my lungs. I throw my leg one final time and impact with his face. Una's screams bash my ears as I try to catch my breath. My body aches and the earlier rush is gone. Now I just feel fucking exhausted.

“What is wrong with you?” Finn’s speaking, and when I glance at him, I see it’s directed toward me.

“So it’s my fault?” I ask him, but I’m aware that Shane is standing up while Una frets over him.

“Is it?”

“What does it matter? I’m wrong no matter what.” I yank my arm free from Finn. Liam has already released me. Mary is standing at the kitchen sink, a cloth clutched to her chest, the water soaking into her white blouse.

“I’m sorry you had to see that Mary,” I say before I leave the room.

CHAPTER FOURTEEN

CIARA

NO MATTER HOW MANY times I try to forget about the two guys, I can't. My mind won't slow down. I keep thinking they'll be waiting for me around every corner. I've started to carry a knife and pepper spray in my bag.

I hesitate as I stuff it into my locker. Should I remove it and take it with me? I push the bag into the locker. I'm no longer working in the strip club. Since the incident, I've been assigned to cleaning rooms only.

A scream tears from my throat as Darragh pops up out of nowhere.

"I don't look that bad," he says around a swollen lip and a black eye.

"Should I ask?" I close the locker door as my heart falls into a steady pattern.

"It was just a family disagreement."

I can't look away from his battered face. "I'd hate to see what happens when your family has a serious row."

"Someone normally dies." The way Darragh says it has me narrowing my eyes at him.

"I'm joking," he says. "So let's start work."

I get my trolley and make my way to our first room. "Are you okay?" He seems to be leaning more so on his right leg.

"You want to nurse me back to health?" His grin returns.

"I think I'll pass." I slide my card into the room door.

The moment we enter, Darragh sits on the floor in his usual spot. "Can I sit this one out? Since I'm injured?"

"You'll have to tell me what happened." I don't really expect him to tell me, and when he looks away, I start to strip the bed.

"The second eldest of us, Shane, he just hates me."

I take a quick peek at Darragh. He's studying his hands, so I continue to clean.

"When we were in school, if anyone annoyed one of us, they had to deal with us all. Family came first, no matter what."

When I steal another glance at Darragh, there's a sad smile on his face.

He shrugs to the floor. "Family still comes first, even though it's all fucked up now. But back then, we really had each other's backs. We were brothers."

I'm so aware of each word, and something is telling me that Darragh doesn't share too much. For me, if anyone asked questions now, I would know they were listening, and I would shut down, so I continue cleaning the room, slowly and quietly to allow him to keep speaking.

"You know, it was all pretty great until our mother died." His brow furrows, and the pain in his eyes has me stopping and breaking my own rules.

"I just lost it..." He looks up at me, and there it is. He knows he's sharing. He shifts.

"Death isn't easy," I say.

He scratches his beard and looks around the room. "I went mad on drugs. I really gave my family a hard time. I don't remember much of it, but I was sent someplace to dry out. My memory is fuzzy. It felt like a prison. It was always so silent and cold."

I'm sitting on the bed now, piecing Darragh together.

"When I came back, everyone was different. Cold. Shane hated me most of all. He said I bailed when they had to face it all. He was right. I took the easy route. It wasn't just us that was different. It was the house, the smell, even the noise."

Darragh trails off, and I find myself on the floor in front of him. The strain on his face barely holds back his pain.

I slowly touch his hand. "I'm so sorry, Darragh," I say. My touch has his eyes flickering up to mine.

"I don't know how to fix anything. I just seem to have a habit of breaking things."

Liam's words about him breaking pretty things floods my mind, and I remove my hand. "Maybe cut back on the drink," I say. "You reek."

He gets off the ground. His hand fills my vision, and I take it as he helps me get up. He doesn't release my hand until my eyes settle on his.

"What about you?"

I can't hold his eye. "What about me?" I easily remove my hand from his and start making the bed.

"I spill my guts out, and you won't tell me about you."

"I didn't force you." I glance at him.

His grin isn't filled with humor. "Fine." He stomps to the cart and gets a polish and duster. The side table is assaulted by his large hands. My heart races in my chest. I don't want him to be mad at me, which is a crazy feeling to have.

"They're dead," I say.

Darragh stops abusing the furniture. "What happened?" My stomach squeezes, and I search the room for words. I don't talk about it.

"My mum overdosed." I keep my head high and wait for the judgment.

"Fuck, that's intense."

"I found her," I blurt out, blood pounding in my ears. Saying it out loud makes it too real.

"My dad was a junkie too. He also overdosed." I'm nodding, just trying to tell myself to keep it together.

"Ciara." The way Darragh says my name has me turning away.

"It's fine," I say quickly as I go to my trolley. I don't know what I'm looking for. I freeze as strong arms wrap around me.

"What are you doing?" Fear clogs my voice.

"Just let me. Please." Darragh turns me in his arms and holds me. I can't respond as my arms hang loosely at my side.

"What are you doing?" My voice trembles again as I keep staring at the door. I won't close my eyes. I can't. If I close my eyes, I don't know what will happen.

"I'm hugging you." He explains to my hair, and God does it feel nice to have this contact. But I don't know what to do with it.

I want to push him away and put my walls back up, but I can't move. My hands seem to rise on their own accord, and I'm wrapping them around his back. I'm all in now, but closing my eyes will break me.

"I've been living on the streets with my father since I was sixteen." I tell this to the door, and Darragh tightens his hold on me. I don't blink. "He died three days after my seventeenth birthday. So I've been on the streets until your brother found me."

A kiss is planted on the top of my head, and I want to ask Darragh to stop. I want my tongue to stop moving, but it doesn't.

"I learned to protect myself. I had to," I whisper.

Too many memories slowly flood my mind, and I close my eyes against them, only to fill up with pain that has me clutching Darragh. I'm a sinking ship and Darragh can't swim. I know losing myself in him is dangerous, but I can't stop the pain. My hands push against his chest as I try to stop this, but he holds me.

"It's okay, Ciara."

"No, it's not. Just let me go."

Darragh does, but I don't step away from him. His frame is a shield from reality. I just need a moment to pull myself together.

"Look at me," he says. I do as tears create a path down my face. "It's okay to let someone in."

My hands still rest on his chest. The heat and the heavy beat of his heart has my own beating to a new dance. One I'm not familiar with. I'm looking at him, and it feels like too much.

Darragh moves closer, dipping his head, and I'm not sure what's happening between us. I don't want to lose myself. He moves closer, his large hands cupping my face as his lips touch mine.

I'm kissing him back with an uncertainty, like he'll change his mind in a second, but he deepens the kiss. I'm moving fast; the air is thinning, and I feel like I'm drunk. I break the kiss. Darragh's heavy breaths brush my face.

"You can't kiss me," I tell his chest. "You can't… just…" I lick the salty moisture from my lips. "Do that. You can't just kiss me." Each breathless word is painful, and I want to lash out. I move away from him, and I can't look up at him. "You have no right."

"You kissed me back." His words have my focus snapping up to him.

Blowing air through my lips, my vision wavers. "This isn't right."

"We're two adults who kissed. Don't make it sound like a crime."

"Don't ever do that again." My angry words come out calmly, and Darragh snorts.

"Fine, Ciara. I was just trying to comfort you."

"By sticking your tongue down my throat," I bark back.

"You're twisting this. You kissed me back." Darragh walks away from me.

"Yeah, well, don't do it again."

He looks at me over his shoulder and shakes his head but doesn't answer me.

"I'm cleaning the bathroom. Alone." I'm stumbling, gathering supplies I don't even look at. Once I close the bathroom door, I move to the sink and run the taps before sinking to the floor. My hands cover my mouth as I try to push everything back in, but it won't go back down. Everything haunts me, all the ghosts. Biting my hand keeps some of the pain at bay. I want to hurt Darragh. Why him? Why the hell did I open up to him?

"Ciara." Darragh's voice and a knock at the door brings me to the surface.

"Five minutes," I choke out, but the door is opening. "Oh my God. Just give me a minute." My lip trembles as I speak.

But he isn't leaving. "I don't know what to do here, Ciara."

"Are you deaf? I said leave. I don't want you here." My anger rises like a tide, and I'm on my feet. The tears stop.

His laugh has my anger boiling over. The blood that pounds through my veins feels red hot. "You find this funny?"

"No." His stupid-ass answer is said with a grin. "I've just never felt this unsure before." It's in his eyes—the pain, the strain he carries daily. He's tired, and just like that, my anger deflates like a burst balloon, and I give a wobbly smile.

"We can pretend today never happened," I say as the lid goes back on my emotions.

"Is that what you really want?"

What kind of question was that? "Yeah, it is."

He nods.

I don't stand around, allowing myself to break again. After splashing my face with water, I pat it. Darragh still stands behind me, and I refuse to meet his eye in the mirror.

"We better get this room finished. It's taking too long." I turn around and face him.

"What if I don't want to pretend today didn't happen?"

"Tough." I move past him, and a part of me lights up as he grips my arm, but another says I'm too tired for the feelings he's making me feel.

I'm waiting for him to speak, and when he doesn't, I glance up at him. Our eyes clash and he releases me.

I finish the room robotically.

The rest of the day is a blur of work. I eat my food, but I don't taste it. I don't pause until the laundry is dropped off in the laundry room. I pretend I don't notice how Darragh hasn't left my side, even as I clock out and make my way down the hall. But as we reach the last hallway, I know I have to say something.

"Why are you following me?" I ask the empty hall in front of me and the looming presence beside me.

"I'm not." He's right, he's not. We're both going to the parking lot.

I root out my phone, remembering I need to ring a taxi.

"I can give you a lift," Darragh says.

I take a quick peek at him, and he isn't looking at me. He seems distant and that comforts me. "Are you sure?"

"I wouldn't offer if I wasn't." This time, he looks at me. His face grows serious.

"Thanks."

His Audi doesn't fit in with all the staff cars. "For a cleaner, you're doing pretty well," I tease.

He grins. "I have other jobs."

I get into his car. "Like what?"

"Stuff that would have you curling up in your bed at night."

It's not what he says but how he looks at me when he mentions my bed. The air catches in my throat, and I put on my belt to distract myself. I'm overthinking everything.

"I didn't picture you doing something gentle," I say.

He starts up the car. "If you had to guess, what do you think?"

I look at Darragh now. He's very well put together—his hair is shiny, his skin flawless. He takes care of his physical self. He could be a personal trainer, but he would be too selfish.

"I don't think you do anything else, only just whatever you want."

"What does that even mean?" He sounds so offended.

I smile as I lean back into the heated seat. "You've always had money. You're a privileged child. You've never had to work for anything. You also wouldn't understand hunger or cold. Those ideas would be foreign to you." Now I look at Darragh. I'm expecting him to be clutching the steering with anger, but he isn't.

"Yeah, that sounds pretty right. But now I've been cut off, so I have to work."

"So the job is covering your Audi payments, tax, insurance, and all that? I don't know where I'm going wrong." My sarcasm has him smiling.

"A wise woman once told me that if a woman can make you smile, then she's a keeper."

I'm not sure how I feel about his statement. "Was it your mother?"

His smile slips. I think I make him frown more than smile, but I keep that to myself.

"No, my cook."

I laugh. "Your cook?"

"What? Mary is the best."

"Yeah. You're privileged," I say.

He grins, but it slips from his face. "Fuck."

I want to ask what's wrong, but I don't. A checkpoint up ahead is waving us down. The guard who meets my eye is Gardaí Brady.

"Fuck is right."

CHAPTER FIFTEEN

DARRAGH

ONCE THE CAR STOPS, I roll down the window.

"License and registration."

I wonder which one of them offered my friends immunity to put me behind bars.

My license falls onto my lap as I flip down the visor. Picking it up, I don't hand it to him straight away. "What's this about?" I ask.

Ciara clears her throat beside me, getting the Gardaí's attention.

"Your license, Darragh." Tom speaks to me while looking at Ciara.

I hand it over to him, and he finally looks away from Ciara and at my license.

"How many of you does it take to read my license? Oh, actually don't tell me," I say to Tom.

His smile holds his secrets, as if I don't know my friends are ready to sell me out.

"Miss Michaels, I see you're keeping some fine company." Tom leans in.

I'm very tempted to roll up the window on his face.

Ciara doesn't answer him, and he leans back out. I'm handed my license back.

"Tell me what they pay you. Five hundred a week, maybe six hundred?" I'm grinning as I turn the key in the ignition.

"You'll get what you deserve soon." Tom taps the hood of my car.

"We'll see. I'll let you lads get back to your minimum watch job while I go home and wipe my ass with one hundred-euro notes." My smile has both of them standing back from the car. I'm waiting to be pulled out and arrested, but when they both stay silent, I know I won't get arrested today.

"See you soon, Darragh." The warning is there in his voice.

I roll up my window and drive off, foot to floor.

"Is that necessary? Are you trying to get arrested?"

I lift my foot off the gas pedal. "They always fucking target me."

"Yes, Darragh. You are such a victim. I mean, you insulted them in every way possible."

I glance at Ciara. "You have no idea what they're like."

"They're the Gardaí. They aren't going to be all friendly."

She has no fucking idea.

"Yeah, you're right," I say to end this conversation.

"Don't be an ass. You don't mean it, so don't say it."

I face the road. "Fine, I fucking hate them."

"At least you're honest."

When I glance at Ciara, her plump lips tug up. I want to kiss them. How had I not noticed her lips before? I keep looking at her. I thought she was pretty from the moment I set eyes on her, but now she's fucking gorgeous. How does that shit happen?

"So are we still good for the wedding?" I ask.

"Yeah. Just remember, I'm not going to sleep with you."

I grin. "Can I put money on it?" When I look at her, she isn't smiling like I expected.

"Do I look like a hoe?"

Fuck. "Of course not."

"Of course not? Like me being a hoe isn't possible?"

I look at her again, wondering if she's messing with me. No. She's serious as fuck.

"You're confusing the fuck out of me, Ciara. You could be a hoe if you wanted. I'd pay."

My words have her shaking her head, and I'm glad when Kingscourt comes into view. No woman has ever made me feel so stupid. I've never questioned myself as much as I do with Ciara. I pull up outside her place, and she's ready to jump out.

"All I'm saying is," I start. "I'd sleep with you."

She pauses and then turns around and kind of smiles. I think it's a smile. It could be a grimace. "A thousand," she says.

"A thousand what?"

"That I don't sleep with you."

I smile while reaching across the open space. "You have to shake on it."

She takes my hand, and I'm tempted to pull her in for a kiss just to see what she would do. Her hand slips from mine quickly, and she closes the door in my face. I watch her until she disappears behind her door.

***

When I arrive home, I'm not expecting a welcome home committee.

"What?" I ask, closing the door behind me. Una's standing in the hall with her arms folded.

"Your dad has called a family meal tonight. You have to be there, no exceptions."

"You mean our dad," I fire back and regret it.

She closes her eyes and shakes her head. "Why do you do that? Sabotage yourself all the time. Are you afraid we might love you?" Una takes a step toward me.

I fold my arms across my chest. "Are you hitting on me?"

"God damn it, Darragh, stop. I'm trying to help you."

"I don't need help. You and Shane do." I don't mean a word I'm saying. But I also don't need an intervention.

"See. I know you don't mean that. You're deflecting."

"Una, I've had a rough fucking day. So can we hit pause on this and pick it up another time?" I'm walking around her and up the stairs.

"Dinner's at eight." Her words follow me all the way up the the landing.

The moment I get into my room, I light a fag. I need a drink. I open the bottom drawer and remove a full bottle of whiskey. I'm staring at the reddish-brown liquid, but all I hear is Ciara telling me not to drink. The bottle is placed back into the drawer.

My bedroom is a bomb scare I try to ignore as I pull my shirt off while trying not to burn it. My phone dings.

What's up, man? Want to hang out? The text is from Art.

I want to smash the phone at his betrayal. Maybe he deserves to die. I put the phone down and head for the bathroom. I throw my fag into the toilet and flush, but it won't disappear. After three flushes, it finally goes down.

Once I'm in the shower, I let my mind wander back to Ciara. She can be my distraction. There's no betrayal from Art or fight with Shane. Connor is still here, and my father isn't an asshole. Right now, there's only Ciara, and she wants me.

Closing my fingers, I take my shaft in my hand and start a slow stroke. I'm picturing Ciara lying on a hotel bed, her blouse open, her black bra full. I try not to go too quickly with my strokes, but my body demands it. I skip ahead until I'm buried inside her.

My pace quickens as I slam my free hand against the tiles. On tippy-toes, I push my body faster as I picture her coming over my cock. My seed sprays the white tiles of the shower. The release allows me to relax and sink back down to my feet. That was good. It was quick, but good.

"Darragh." Finn steps into the bathroom.

"I could have been jerking off," I say while firing a look over my shoulder.

"Are you?" Disgust fills his voice.

I rinse myself down. "No. But can't I have a fucking minute?"

"Sorry, I'll wait in your bedroom."

I finish my wash quickly and get out of the shower.

"I'm very popular today," I say when I enter my room. Finn is sitting on my unmade bed.

"Did you talk to Shane?"

I run the towel across my head. "No, Una was waiting for me when I got home. Why, does Shane want to make up?" I grin as I search for clean clothes.

"What's going on with you?" Finn's decent, and I know his concern is genuine. I'd normally tell him. But his wedding is a few days away.

"I drank too much last night. I'll make up with Shane." The relief is immediate on Finn's face.

"Thank you." He exhales heavily.

I turn and drop the towel. The boxers and jeans go on quickly, and I turn back around.

"No problem. So, we're having a family meal?" I get out a new black shirt. May as well get some wear out of them. Pulling off the tags, I check myself in the mirror.

"Yeah, I think Dad just wants to warn us all to be on our best behavior for my wedding."

"You mean warn me." I meet Finn's eyes in the mirror.

He can't hold my stare. "Please, Darragh. Don't make this about you."

What the fuck did that mean? "I'll be on my best behavior."

"Like I haven't heard that before." This time, Finn's voice carries a playful tone. "I'll see you downstairs."

Once Finn leaves my room, I sit on my bed with my phone. I don't feel like pretending tonight, but I have to.

What's up? I'm good. Just hungover. Having a family thing tonight, so I'll have to skip. Might have drinks tomorrow night. Maybe just us two like old times.

Once I send the message to Art, I get on my shoes and socks before leaving my room.

No one is in the dining room yet, so I head for the kitchen. I'm starving and the smell that wafts from it has me heading in that direction.

"Mary." I kiss her on the cheek.

She smiles up at me. "Are you okay?" It's whispered, and that's when I see Una and Shane sitting at the kitchen table. I can't stop the smile that spreads across my face. Shane looks far worse than me.

"I'm okay. You should see the other guy."

Mary giggles, then remembers herself and gives me a half-arsed stern look.

I sit down across from Una and Shane. Una stiffens, but Shane stares at me like the devil just sat down.

"I'm sorry about today," I say to Shane. Una's eyes light up. She wraps her hand around Shane's open fingers and squeezes like she's trying to get a response out of him.

"It's not me you need to apologize to. It's Una."

"I'm sorry, Una," I say to her.

"I forgive you." She smiles wide. Shane doesn't, but he doesn't look ready to kill me at least.

"Okay, all into the dining room." Mary ushers us out of the kitchen. "I'm ready to start dishing this out shortly."

"Wish me luck," I say to Mary, and expect her to smile at me, but I'm surprised when she makes me stay behind.

"You don't need luck, Darragh. You're the kindest of them all. Don't keep letting them hurt you."

Her words have me kissing her softly on the cheek.

"As kind as Finn?" I ask with a raised eyebrow.

She smiles. "Always with the last word." She returns to the stove.

I pause at the door. "Thanks, Mary."

"For what?" She's smiling sweetly at me.

"For believing in me."

"Always, Darragh."

Everyone's in the room when I enter. It's always the same set up. Liam to Father's right, Shane to his left. This time, Una sits beside Shane—that's my spot—and Finn sits beside Liam. I opt to sit beside Una, so I don't have direct sight of Shane.

"I'm glad everyone came." Father raises his glass.

Not everyone, I think as I pour a glass of water. Connor isn't here. When I look up, I wonder if I've spoken out loud.

"What?" Shit, I hope I hadn't.

"Nothing." Una speaks up and fires a stern eye around the room.

As I lift the glass, Finn smiles. I stare at the glass in my hand, and it dawns on me. Everyone is staring at me because I'm having a glass of water.

"I'm just trying it out," I tell them, and a part of me hates how fucking proud they all look, especially Finn.

"Maybe you could consider not drinking the day of Finn's wedding." Father's voice rings clear across the room.

Bang. There we go. All I need to do is remain calm.

"I'll give it a try," I say in a big fuck-you voice.

"We would all really appreciate that." His words are clipped as he sips his wine.

"You don't have to do that," Finn says.

I take a gulp of my water. "I don't mind."

"He does have to do it, Finn. Darragh is too unpredictable with alcohol. You don't want him ruining your wedding."

My eyes snap to my father, and I'm wondering if he's trying to start a row. He focuses on Finn like I'm even not here.

"He said he would try, so let's take his word for it." Liam speaks up, and he meets everyone's gaze before stopping at me. A curt nod from him, and the conversation about me fucking everything up ends.

I want to ruin this meal for my father. I'm considering bringing up Connor. I know that will kick off a row.

"Where's Connor?" Una asks innocently from beside me.

I smirk.

"He's working," Father says, and smiles sweetly at Una.

"He got a job?" I ask.

My father lands his full stare on me. "He has a job just like the rest of you."

"Father is trying to cover up something that doesn't need to be covered up." Liam meets my eye before speaking to Una. "Connor struggles with the family. He wanted space, so we gave it to him. He's safe and fine, and we will all catch up at the wedding."

I take a peek at Una, and she's drinking up his lies like it's a fine wine.

I wonder when we became so good at lying to other people and each other. I glance at Finn, and his clenched face and hard eyes tell me he knows what really happened. Connor must have told him. When he looks at me, my stomach twists with guilt.

"I met him recently and he's fine," I say to Una, but I'm also telling Finn. I need him to know that things are fine between me and Connor.

"What did you do?" Finn asks, and it's like he knows I asked Connor to help me hurt someone.

"Just hung out with some friends." Art's betrayal is there in the front of my mind. I'm glancing at Liam and find him watching me. I have to tell him what happened, but not until after the wedding.

"So is Siobhan all set for the wedding?" Una slides in her question with a smile, and the conversation shifts to a comfortable ground. The wedding becomes everyone's focus. Mary brings in our dinner, and it's the only redeeming thing about this meal. I feel like everyone is watching me, waiting for me to fuck up by either saying something inappropriate or taking a drink. So I eat and keep my lips sealed.

"I can't wait until you see her in her dress, Finn. She's going to blow your mind."

"She blows my mind anyway." Finn's smiling like a drunken sailor, and I'm happy for him.

When I look at Liam, I don't see happiness at all. He knows I'm watching him; his eyes meet mine, and it's me who looks away.

"Before the wedding, I just wanted to say a few words." Father rises and takes his glass with him.

"The day you were born, we nearly lost your mother. I remember being called in. The chaos in the room was frightening, but then you cried and everything melted away for a moment. Big blue eyes looked up at me and you stopped, Finn."

I'm wondering where I was since me and Finn are fucking twins.

"Your mother believed she was going to die, and she just asked me to promise her that I would love and care for you all." His eyes touch each of us, and I want to salute him for failing fucking miserably.

"Thankfully, she pulled through and raised you all. I'm not sure what way you would have turned out otherwise. I'm proud of you, Finn." He holds his glass higher, and everyone follows suit.

"You've always been a good son, a good brother, and now you will be a great husband." Father drinks and we all do the same to close the speech.

"To family. May it always come first."

I'm already getting sick of drinking water. A beer would wash his bullshit down.

Una's clapping beside me like a happy fucking seal. I grin when I look at Finn. He's so happy with Father's praise.

The conversation continues about the wedding, and I'm glad when Mary arrives in with dessert. This is coming to an end.

CHAPTER SIXTEEN

CIARA

"So you still good to go to the wedding tomorrow?" Darragh's been asking me the same question the last few days like I'm going to back out of it. I've thought about not going, but things have fallen into a comfortable pattern with us.

We work together, have lunch, and Darragh drops me home and picks me up. I enjoy his company, and we haven't mentioned the kiss. Yet I can't seem to forget about it.

"Yes. So when do I get to see my dress?"

He grins at me as he puts on a fresh pillowcase. He's still using my rubber gloves, which are way too small for his large hands. "You can try it on for me after work."

Going to the cart and getting polish and a duster gives me a moment to hide my burning face. The idea of Darragh standing in my apartment does funny things to my stomach. "You'll just have to wait until tomorrow."

"Fine. When I drop you home, I'll give it to you. I have it in the car."

"It better fit, or I'll have to wear my trousers and a shirt." I'm teasing.

Darragh puts the final pillow on the bed. "If you want to wear your trousers, I'm cool with that. Whatever you're comfortable with." He's being serious.

"Nah, I never get to dress up."

We move onto the next room. Thinking about the wedding tomorrow is making me nervous. The sad reality is I've never been to one. I've never worn a dress. I don't share this with Darragh. I don't want to make a big deal out of it.

"So… my family is pretty intense." Darragh isn't looking at me; instead, he's checking the wardrobes to make sure the previous guests didn't leave anything behind. His tense shoulders and the fact he won't look at me tells me that he's worried. "They don't agree with my lifestyle and pretty much think I'm going to fuck it up. So if they start, you have to ignore them." He closes the wardrobes.

"Okay."

Darragh looks at me, searching my face. "Okay."

"I don't think you're going to fuck anything up." I'm finding it hard to meet his eye. I believe what I'm saying, and that confuses me. Since when do I believe in someone?

"Trust me. If anyone will make a mess of the wedding, it will be me. So I'm going to try not to drink."

Darragh moves toward me, and my heart rate picks up. He makes me feel small, and with each step, my breath lodges in my throat. Is he going to kiss me? Would I stop him?

Darragh's eyes shine, and his lips tug up slightly as he leans around me. When he moves back, he's holding a pair of blue gloves. I die a little as he grins like he knows what I was thinking and knows the effect he just had on me. He moves away and starts stripping the bed. I pick up my brain and lady parts off the floor. What the hell is wrong with me?

"I won't drink either," I say as I strip the quilt. I can feel Darragh's focus on me, and when I look up, it's confirmed.

"You don't have to do that."

"I know," I answer.

He seems stunned for a moment. "It's going to be one boring wedding with both of us sober."

I tut. "With me, I'm a joke a minute. I don't need a drink."

Darragh's grin reappears.

After work, Darragh keeps to his word and drives me home. Once we reach the apartment, he hands me a bag that has my dress and shoes in it.

"Thanks." I wrap my arms around it. I'm so nervous to see what he picked for me.

"If you need help with your hair or makeup, just let me know."

"What, you have more hidden talents?"

Darragh laughs at my remark. "My stepsister would gladly help."

My stomach flips at the idea of his sister helping me. I shake my head. "I'm good, but thanks."

"So I'll pick you up around twelve in the morning."

"I'll be ready." My nerves are kicking in. I can feel the tremble rise all the way into my hands, so before I start shaking, I get out of the car and don't look back.

Peaches is waiting for me when I enter my apartment. I rush to get her some food and milk before bringing the bag into the bedroom. I'm staring at it, afraid to look. I hate how much this means to me. I want to savor every second of the unwrapping. My first dress and I let a guy pick it.

"Here goes," I tell myself as I open the bag.

The dress I pull out has my pulse spiking. It's a blue I see all the time. It's the same as my eyes. I've often been told they're electric blue. The satin runs over my hands. The full-length dress had a generous slit that goes up my thigh while the halter neck has a plunge line. It's stunning. But for me, I'm not so sure.

The doorbell ringing has me placing the dress onto the bed before returning to the living room.

"Hello?" I speak into the intercom.

"Hi, Ciara, it's Bernie."

"Come on up." I buzz Bernie in and open the door.

I've never met her before, but as she rounds the corner, I notice she's a lot younger than I thought she would be. Her buzz-cut hairstyle and baggy clothes aren't what I expected from a hairdresser.

"Hi, Bernie," I greet her as she reaches the top step.

"How do you climb so many steps?" She's puffing as she steps into the apartment.

"I suppose I just got used to them." I'm nervous about getting my hair done.

"So I'm going to set up here. Is that okay?" Bernie asks as she places her bag on the counter.

"Work away."

"Are you sure about this?" She smiles.

I sit down on the chair she points to and let her remove my hair tie.

"Yes. I think so." I'm smiling too.

"What's your natural color?" she asks while parting my hair. "Ah, I see it's blonde." The blue is starting to leave my roots, showing some of my natural color.

"Yeah white blonde. Can you remove all the blue?"

"I can do anything. Just relax and let me work my magic."

***

It takes three hours, and when Bernie is finished, I'm starving and a little surprised with how I look. I'm in the bathroom mirror, and it's been so long since I saw *me*. The me that I hide from the world.

My stomach twists, and I want my blue hair back. It was the thing that made me stand out but also made me look dangerous, a warning not to mess with me. Now I look innocent, and innocent attracts the wrong kind of people. That's why I changed my appearance so much. No makeup, blue hair, baggy clothes, so I'm not worth looking at.

My looks before had brought so much unwanted attention, and not one ounce of it was good. My reflection disappears as I close my eyes and try to take some calming breaths. I'm going to be fine. I'd be with Darragh, after all.

My smile is shaky, but it's there as I picture him seeing me with blonde hair. Blue eyes that look larger stare back at me.

My phone pulls me away from my reflection.

Do you like the dress? Need a hand getting in or out of it?

I picture him in a mansion surrounded by servants or maybe at a party with the elite. If he was, he wouldn't be texting me. So maybe he's just bored.

It's nice.

I go back to the bag and remove the dress again. It causes a lump to rise in my throat. It's stunning. The shoes are also electric blue, with some stones placed at the front where the material gathers.

Just nice??? I picked it myself.

The idea that Darragh selected my dress causes my stomach to tighten.

It's stunning. Thank you, Darragh.

The reply is immediate and makes me smile. **Can't wait to see you in it, blue.**

He won't be able to call me blue anymore. My fingers run through my hair again. It's going to take a while before I get used to the new me. Well, actually, the old me. I look like my mother. The longer I stare at myself, the blurrier my vision grows.

Peaches rubs up against my leg. After rubbing my eyes, I pick her up and focus on her instead.

DARRAGH

We never had a stag for Finn—he didn't want one—but tonight we're meeting up in Cabra Castle for a few drinks, all organized by Liam. He has a big pull there. He hosts most of his 'private' meetings there. He could own the place for all I know. Liam is a closed book, like always.

"You got an invitation?" I say with a smirk, when I spot Connor at the front desk.

He grins when he sees me. "I'm doing this for Finn," he says, moving away from the desk.

"Me too. I could think of lots of other places I want to be."

Glancing around the area, I see we're the only one's here. "Are you early? Or are they late?"

"They're upstairs. I said I'd wait for you."

"The wait is over." I'm waiting for it, and it doesn't take long. I've only got my foot on the first step when Connor speaks.

"Don't forget you have to talk to Liam or I will."

"Fuck's sake, Connor. I know. Why does everyone feel the need to babysit me?"

I don't expect his laughter. "Because you know you need someone to look out for you. You're a loose cannon." When Connor says it, it's with humor and not the vindictive way I'm used to hearing it from the rest.

"Well, you'll be glad to know I haven't touched a drink in six days."

Connor throws me a sideways glance as we head up the stairs. "It's a girl, isn't it?"

We reach the second floor and walk past a tin man that would creep me out if I wasn't sober.

"No, I'm just sick of listening to people's shit," I say.

He grins. "Nope, we've been at you your whole life, so why now?"

Is he right? Is it Ciara? No. It's to shut my father the fuck up.

"I'm sick of always being the disappointment."

Connor stops walking and grips my shoulder. "Don't ever say that again. I know you might think that, but they all think a lot of you. Why do you think they protect you so much? If they didn't care, they'd say nothing, like they do with me."

"What's this, see who Father hates the most?" I joke.

"He's not my father." Connor's serious tone has us walking again, and I'm glad when we reach the private room. I'm also glad when I see it's just us brothers.

Finn's face lights up when he sees Connor, and he embraces him like he hasn't seen his brother in ages. I look at Liam, wondering if he'll reconsider the ban he put on Connor.

Finn slaps me on the back. "You guys are so late." He sits down, and I check my phone.

"By twenty minutes," I say and pour out a glass of water. This time, no one says anything.

"A toast to Finn, the first of us to marry. He may also be the last." Connor makes the speech, not caring about how Liam and Shane watch him.

I join in. "Last night of freedom. You can always run now," I tell Finn.

He smiles. "I'm good," he says and we drink.

"So what's on the menu tonight?" I ask Liam since he organized this. When he lifts the menu, I sneer.

"I was talking about entertainment. Did you bring anything home from work?"

"Finn wouldn't approve." Liam continues to stare at the food menu.

Finn looks sheepish "What? I don't want that."

"Yeah, but what about the rest of us?" I ask.

"There's only you and Liam."

I can't even look at Liam. I'm not sure what he's into—men, women, maybe both, maybe none. He shows no interest. But now my interest is piqued.

"You want to hit a strip joint later, brother?"

Liam's lips twitch. "You seem to forget I own several."

Finn steers the conversation away from strippers and back to us. It's nice to have just us brothers here. No matter how much we fight or hurt each other, we all come back to each other in the end. We all protect each other. Family comes first, no matter what.

CHAPTER SEVENTEEN

DARRAGH

It's the morning of the wedding, and my stomach tightens and twists. I need a drink. I'm fixing my tie and failing each time when a knock sounds on my room door.

"Come in," I call, not looking away from the mirror as I pull the tie off for the hundredth time and try to retie it. I pause when I meet my father's eye in the mirror.

"I'm still sober. No need to check up on me." It's out of my mouth before I remember who I'm speaking to. "Sorry," I add quickly.

He nods. "I'm not here to check up on you, but it's great to see you're sober."

I turn around, and Father walks toward me. He's a large man. Even at his age, he still scares the crap out of me.

"Let me fix your tie. Your mother taught me." He speaks while he places the tie around my neck.

I'm uncomfortable waiting for him to tighten it until it cuts off my air supply. Sweat gathers between my shoulder blades as I watch his hands move. He doesn't strangle me; he just makes the knot in my tie.

"I know what you did. As do other people." The knot moves into place a little too tightly, and when I clear my throat, he loosens it. "It's important that you don't say anything out of place. These people will hang us the moment we step out of line."

Father steps back and brushes my shoulders. "You've grown into a man," he says, but my mind is stuck on what he's saying.

"I don't know..."

"It's your brother's wedding. I don't want to hurt you. So just listen and shut up. You know what I'm talking about. Unless you've been up to worse than robbing banks like you're some low-life criminal."

The blood drains from me, but I hold myself firm.

"Just give your family this one day."

I nod.

His hand lands with some force across my face, patting my cheek. I don't move until he leaves my room.

I loosen the tie straight away before going to the back of my wardrobe and removing a small bag of coke I keep hidden. My hands are sweaty as I take it to my bed. I pat my jacket pocket and remove my wallet. Rolling up a fifty, I take out my card. A knock at my door has me sitting on top of my stash.

"What do you think?" It's Finn. He does a twirl.

"The suits okay, but that face blows my fucking mind."

He grins while checking himself out in the mirror. His gray suit is tailored to perfection, the same as all of us. We're all in gray with a white shirt to tie in with Siobhan's dress.

As he checks himself out, I'm hoping nothing's stuck to my ass. I grab everything and stuff it into my pocket and wipe my bed quickly. I'm sweating as I turn to Finn.

"Are you nervous?" I ask him.

He looks away from the mirror, his eyes trailing around my room. His brows furrow deeply. "I think I'm more nervous that your room is clean."

"You and me both." Being off the drink gives me too much time on my hands.

"Let's hope she shows up," I say.

Finn widens his eyes. "Don't say that, man."

Like it was a possibility.

He swallows his nerves. "We better head down."

"I'll see you at the church. I've got to pick up my date." I don't look at him as I speak.

"Yeah, this mysterious date. Did you pay her?"

"I kind of did," I say honestly.

Finn's face falls. "You're bringing a prostitute to my wedding?"

I'm laughing at the insult. Ciara would hit him for that one. "No. But I had to bribe her to come with me. She wasn't exactly on board."

"But she's coming willingly?"

"Ha ha." We leave the room and part ways. He's joining Shane and Liam in the study, so I don't envy him.

The minute I'm outside, I light a fag and just sit on the steps, letting the air cool me down. The front door opens and Liam steps out. I want to roll my mother fucking eyes.

"I've already been warned. So don't start."

He pauses on the steps. "I'm just going to get the car."

I take a deep drag of my fag.

Liam watches me. "What did he say to you?"

That he knows I robbed a bank. "Just not to drink," I say, standing up. My movement causes the small bag of white powder to fall onto the step. We both look at it.

"I wasn't going to use it." I stare at the bag.

Liam bends at the waist and picks it up. "Good. You won't need it, then."

I say nothing as he slips it into his pocket and walks away. A part of me feels lighter to have the temptation out of my way. But it has also made me feel better knowing it was in arm's reach if I wanted it.

"Fuck." I throw my smoke onto the ground and go get my car. I need to pick up Ciara.

***

Ciara isn't like other girls. When I ring and tell her I'm outside, her door opens. She doesn't keep me waiting. A woman steps out wearing Ciara's dress, and I can't look away. A blonde bombshell, but it's the eyes that I've looked at every day that has me realizing it's Ciara. The keys rattle in my hand as I pull them from the ignition and get out.

Ciara looks at me from under her thick black eyelashes, making her look so innocent. So beautiful. She's something to protect. But from firsthand experience, I know that's not true. She's well capable of protecting herself. She always had an air of innocence about her. Before, it was buried under a smart mouth and anger; now, there's nothing to hide it.

I watch her as I move around the car and meet her at the door. The rise and fall of her chest shows how nervous she is. The plunging line showcases perfectly firm breasts.

"I have an idea," I say and she smiles, but it's strained. I've never seen her this nervous. "Let's go back inside so I can peel that dress off you."

She laughs, and it does the job I intended it to do. It makes her relax. "I'm never sleeping with you." Her comeback doesn't hold the normal amount of belief it normally does.

I really want to tell her how amazing she looks, but that would scare her off.

"So that's a no, then?"

"Yes, it's a no." She's still smiling, and a light blush kisses her cheeks.

"Are you sure?"

She laughs again and nods. Stepping aside, I open the car door for her and she slides in. The dress splits open, and I see so much fucking skin. The cold metal of the car door is the only thing that keeps me from leaning in and kissing her. I focus on the feel of the door.

"I'm in," she tells me.

I've been standing here too long. After closing the car door, I race around to my side and slide in.

"You look really good." Her words have me grinning.

I fire up the car. "I know," I tell her as I pull out and she smiles. "You look good too." Her smile isn't as wide, so I keep any further compliments to myself.

I can't stop stealing glances at her. "Who knew you were blonde."

She touches her hair. "What, this? No. I'm naturally blue. Just thought I could do with a bit of a change."

"Well, it suits you. I think you look hot." I kick myself for letting it slip, but she smiles up at me.

"Really?" She isn't fishing for a compliment. She really doesn't know how gorgeous she is.

"I'd sleep with you," I say and my heart beats faster. I mean it, and something in her posture tells me she's picked up that this time it's different.

"That's an odd compliment. But thank you."

"You don't want to return the compliment. Tell me how you're undressing me with your eyes."

Her laughter fills my car. That's what I've been doing since I saw her—undressing her with my eyes.

"Yes, I can't stop picturing you naked."

"Oh, tell me more," I tease. The blush on her cheeks makes me wonder if she really is picturing me naked.

We pull into Kells, and I don't drive down to the church grounds knowing parking isn't possible. Instead, I park at the back of the Headfort Arms Hotel. It's another one of Liam's establishments.

I check my watch. It's a quarter to one. The wedding starts at one.

"So I have to go up top with my family, as I'm one of the groomsmen, but I'll leave you with Una."

"You don't have to do that." She looks so pure, making me want to taint that purity with a kiss.

"I know." I get out and move around the car to open her door. Once she's out, I pull the shawl around her shoulders.

"Thank you for doing this for me."

Ciara holds my gaze before reaching up and brushing her lips to my cheek. "You're welcome." The words are whispered against my ear.

I reach out my arm, and Ciara takes it as we leave the parking lot and make our way across the road to the church. The lot is as packed as I expected. With four hundred guests, the church will be full. Some people are still outside smoking or having a last-minute chat. I spot my Father having words with a man who looks similar to him, Uncle Tom. The words are heated but controlled. They wouldn't let themselves down in front of a crowd.

I grip Ciara tighter as I make my way into the church. The walk up the aisle is long, and the seats are filled with a lot of people I don't know but who seem to know me. Being identical to the groom is a bit of a giveaway. I get a lot of nods, smiles, and hellos. Occasionally, someone knows my name.

Liam, Shane, Connor, and Finn are standing at the front of the church. "Those four guys at the altar are my brothers."

"Jesus Christ, you all look like models."

Surprise at her words has me looking down at her. "You think I look like a model?"

She grins up at me but doesn't answer. Liam spots us first, and his eyes slide to Ciara. I see it the moment it happens—the moment he recognizes her. His eyes snap to mine and he nods. I'm not sure if it's approval of who's with me or just the fact that I showed up. Una's fiery red hair is like a siren. She's only three people in and close to the top.

I stop at her row of seats. "Una, this is my date, Ciara. Can I leave her in your hands?" Una takes in Ciara, and she smiles at her. "You can sit with me and Ava."

Ava gives me a smile.

"Nice to see you again," I tell her, and Una seems surprised that we know each other. Beside the three girls is an older woman who is watching us. Most certainly not Liam's date. I'm curious about who he brought.

"You okay?" I ask Ciara before I have to leave.

"Yes, I'm fine. Go on." Her smile has me making a quick decision. I lean in and plant a soft quick kiss on her lips. She looks startled as I leave her and join my brothers.

"You're cutting it close." I ignore Shane's words and pull Finn into a quick hug.

"You can still bail," I tease.

He grins, but it's strained. "Not a chance. I just hope she shows up." He's watching the door like her not arriving would actually happen.

Liam steps closer to me. "You brought Ciara?"

I don't look at him as I speak. "Yes, she cleans up nicely, doesn't she?"

"That she does." I don't like Liam agreeing with me. He steps away as I turn to him.

"You brought the rings?" Connor asks me, and I'm shaking my head, my spine tightening.

"No, what? No one said for me to bring the fucking rings." I'm getting loud, but I didn't fuck this up.

Shane shakes his head at me, but Connor is grinning. "Of course you didn't. I'm the best man."

I want to punch him.

Shane leans in a little too close. "Could you try to watch your mouth? We're standing in a church."

"Move back before I deck you," I say to him through a smile.

"Please remember this is Finn's day." Liam speaks up while glancing out over the crowd.

Finn is staring at the altar, and I nudge Connor. "You're the best man," I whisper, and he steps toward Finn and whispers a few words in his ear.

Music starts and every head whips to the closed front doors.

My own stomach goes for Finn. Taking our places quickly, I find Ciara watching me and I wink at her. The doors open and Siobhan steps in.

I take a quick look at Finn. Tears brim in his eyes as he stares at Siobhan. A veil covers her face, but the dress is stunning, with a train two meters back that has four girls lifting and fixing it at each step she takes.

Father is giving her away. He walks with an air of a man who knows his worth. Head held high, he nods to people as he passes them. When he gets closer to us, he looks at each son, and pride shines in his eyes. I smile as Siobhan reaches Finn, and when he gets to push back the veil, his face transforms as their eyes meet.

The mass is an hour long, and I spend most of my time watching Ciara. She's crying along with Una and Ava. When she meets my eye, I suppress the smile that threatens to appear.

"I now pronounce you husband and wife." The words are music to my ears. The mass is finally over. Finn doesn't waste a minute before he takes Siobhan in his hands and kisses her. The church erupts in cheers.

The bells ring as Finn and Siobhan walk hand in hand down the aisle. A hand lands on my back. It's Connor. "Thank God that's over," he whispers and I agree.

I can't wait for a smoke. As we follow behind, Ava falls into step with Connor and Una with Shane. Ciara looks unsure, but I hold out my hand and she takes it, slipping out of her seat. I check behind me, but Liam walks on his own.

"That was beautiful." Ciara's voice is still clogged with emotion.

"Yeah, it was long," I say.

She squeezes our linked hands. "You can't say that didn't do something to you." She's really emotional, and it's sweet.

"It made me realize I'm really addicted to fags. And I don't like staying in one spot too long."

Ciara narrows her eyes at me.

"Fine, it was beautiful," I say, and she seems satisfied as we step out into the sun. Connor and Ava come over to us.

"Ciara, this is my brother Connor and his girlfriend, Ava." Connor takes Ciara's outstretched hand. Ava and Ciara smile at each other.

"We already met," Ava says.

"Thanks for letting me sit with you."

"I'm as new as you. This is my first time meeting the family." The girls move closer together, bonding over being new.

"I see Liam doesn't have a date," I say to Connor as I spark up a fag.

"I didn't see him come in with anyone. Makes you really wonder about him."

I'm nodding. "Did you see Uncle Tom is here? Father was having words with him earlier."

Connor doesn't look at me as he speaks; his eyes scan across the crowd. "I didn't see him, but they have a bad history, so I'm not surprised."

"Over the shooting?"

Ava and Ciara look up at us. "The bird shooting," I tell them with a smile.

"Here comes Father," I say to Connor and his face tightens. "I mean Michael," I say just for him, and he relaxes.

"Well done. You both did a great job," he tells us. I know we are the fuckups.

"Thanks," I say.

Connor doesn't speak, and I'm grateful that he doesn't. He normally has nothing good to say.

"Are you going to introduce me to your dates?" Father smiles, and he looks like such a sweet and doting father.

"This is Ciara. Ciara, my father." Ciara takes Dad's outstretched hand.

"So great to meet you." Her smile is sweet, and she blinks up at him.

"And this is?" he questions, releasing Ciara's hand. Connor isn't speaking.

"Ava, Connor's girlfriend," I say.

Father steps toward her. "Isn't he a very lucky man?" Father says while taking her hand.

She looks nervously at Connor. His silence isn't helping.

"Okay, family photo, Darragh." Father walks away, and I hate that he got a dig in. How he didn't mention Connor.

"He's such a fucking asshole," I mutter.

"I know, man. But just for Finn, let's make today go smoothly." Connor gives Ava a quick kiss.

"I won't be long," I say to Ciara, wondering what the hell she's making of our family, but she smiles like today is a great day.

An hour of photos and repositioning is bad enough, but with crowds watching us, it's draining.

Three photographers are directing us.

"Okay, can we just have the brothers?"

We all stand together. "Maybe move closer and wrap your arms around each other." We do as instructed. "Now Darragh look at Shane, Liam face forward, and Finn, you look at Connor."

We do that. I'm looking at Shane and its all kinds of awkward.

"On the count of three, say something to each other. One, two, three."

"You're a prick," I say to Shane as the cameras snap away. I'm smiling at him, his face rigid. "That's going to make a great photo," I say as we finally finish up.

"Why didn't you smile?" Una questions Shane, and I'm grinning as I step away.

"What did you say to him?" Connor asks.

"I just said to smile. But he refused."

Connor snorts.

CHAPTER EIGHTEEN

CIARA

I CAN'T TAKE MY eyes off Darragh. He just seems to draw me in. Watching the photoshoot is captivating. Each brother looks like they're modeling wedding clothes. Each one is so different but equally good-looking. Normally, there's an ugly one in the family. But not the O'Reagans.

"So have you and Darragh been together for long?" The question has been asked several times, but I smile at Una. She hadn't asked yet, but I knew she was dying to know.

"We're friends."

Both her eyebrows raise and she smiles. "Ah."

I want to ask what 'Ah' means, but Darragh is walking toward us. A part of me is still reeling from the kiss he gave me in front of everyone. It distracted me and I just couldn't fully enjoy my very first wedding. My lips still tingle, and I wonder why he did it. The first kiss we had was me in tears, telling him my past, but this time he didn't have to kiss me.

"We can start making our way to Cabra." Darragh lights up a cigarette.

"I'm starving and honestly these shoes are cutting into my heels." Una winces as she speaks.

"Yeah, mine too. I should have gotten smaller heels," Darragh says.

Una narrows her eyes at Darragh before smiling at me. "See you at the castle."

Shane arrives then. He doesn't smile much, and he levels Darragh with a stare. I find myself taking a step toward Darragh, not liking his hostility at all. His eyes snap to me and his face softens.

"Can't wait to see the photos. They might have to edit you out." Darragh's words are delivered with a smirk.

Shane's face tightens again. "See you at the castle." He turns and Una gives us an apologetic look.

"So she's your stepsister?" I ask.

Darragh blows smoke into the air. "Yep."

"And he's your brother. So she's also his stepsister?"

"You're preaching to the choir."

"I'm not saying there's anything wrong with it. I'm just curious," I say, not wanting to judge. They aren't related. It's just the title that makes it seem kind of weird.

"I didn't get to meet your date." I startle as Finn comes up behind us. He's Darragh's identical twin, but the more I look at him, I don't think he's like Darragh at all. He's too soft and polished.

"This is Ciara. Ciara, Finn."

"Lovely to meet you, and congratulations."

He smiles sweetly. "Great to meet you too, Ciara. We're going to go to the hotel now. I'd say everyone is starving."

I was hungry, but I didn't say. Finn pats his brother on the back, and we leave together.

"Why did you kiss me?" I ask as we wait to cross the road. Keeping my focus on the traffic allows me the bravery of asking the question.

Once we get safely across the road, Darragh speaks. "Did you like it?"

"You can't answer my question with a question," I tell him.

"I wanted to." He shrugs and throws his fag onto the ground like it's no big deal. Like he didn't leave me stunned and thinking about it through the whole ceremony.

We reach the car, and Darragh opens my door but stands in the way. "Can I do it again?"

My heart starts to race. I want him to do it so much, but I'm scared.

"I think we should keep this platonic." My words don't tether him at all.

His smile is slow. "I think it's a bit too late for that."

Yeah, it is.

He steps aside, and I get into the car.

***

I've never been to Cabra Castle before, but already, it's stolen words from me. This is like a fairy tale. "So, this isn't my doing, but rooms were booked for each of us."

I unbuckle my belt. "Okay?"

"I mean, couple wise. We're sharing a room."

"Oh." The idea of sharing a room with Darragh is heating up my blood.

"Look, I'll sleep on the floor. Scout's honor." Darragh crosses his heart like I might believe him.

"Or we could just ask for a spare bed to be brought in," I say.

"I can organize that."

I grin. "No, let me." I don't trust him one bit.

"So about this platonic relationship. What are the rules?"

"What do you mean rules?" I'm smiling.

Darragh's eyes light up. "Like, can we dance?"

"I won't be dancing, because I can't," I reply.

"But we can dance?"

I laugh. "Yes. We can dance."

"Hand holding?"

"Depends on what the situation is."

His lips tug up into a smile. "A kiss on the cheek?"

"Acceptable."

Darragh moves in and my heart gallops, my grin dissolving off my face. The smell of his cologne fills my lungs, and I can't look away from him. His lips graze my cheek, warm breath brushing my neck, and I shiver. Moist lips touch my neck, and it takes a lot of control to stay still. Each kiss he plants moves closer to my lips. If he reaches them, I'm not sure I can stop him.

A knock on the window has me jumping away from Darragh. He doesn't move away but groans before turning to his window, where his brother Connor grins at him. The burn of embarrassment rushes across my cheeks.

"The happy couple is about to arrive," he informs Darragh before looking at me and grinning.

The heat travels across my chest, and I'm glad when the cool wind blows around me as I step out of the car. Warm fingers wrap around mine, and my head snaps up to Darragh.

"You said hand holding was okay."

"I said it depended on the situation," I answer as I allow myself to relax into his touch.

"So I made an executive decision and decided this was the perfect situation."

We join everybody else as Siobhan and Finn arrive. White petals are lifted by the wind and swirl around the couple. I can't stop looking. There's such a magical feel to it. Regret at not going to a wedding before rises inside me. I never knew what I was missing out on.

Men on either side of the door play the tin whistle, the sound romantic but haunting. The castle inside is even more enchanting. The money this must have cost... I can't even begin to think about it.

Once we enter the main room, I'm separated from Darragh. He has to sit at the head table with the rest of his family, but I've been placed with Ava, and since she's 'new' too, we stick together.

We're seated with mostly Northern Ireland people. Their accents fascinate me. I could listen to them for hours.

"How do you know the bride or groom?" The place name in front of the man is Tom. He looks very similar to Darragh's father, and I wonder if they're related.

"I'm here with Darragh. He's the groom's brother."

"Ah, Darragh, nice bloke. They sure have some fine women down this end of the water."

I grin at the compliment. "Thanks."

"What about you, love?" he asks Ava, and I take the time to start on my soup.

"I'm here with my boyfriend, Connor, also a brother to the groom." It's funny how Ava's response gets everyone's attention.

"You're Connor's woman?" a young lad asks.

"Matt, watch your tongue." Tom's response is sharp, and Matt apologizes to Ava.

It's awkward, but Ava waves it off. I'm glad when the meal part is over and we no longer have to stay at the same tables. My heart lifts as Darragh makes his way over to our table.

"You want to check out the room?" he asks me in front of everyone. Darragh focuses on my company, and he smiles at Tom.

"Uncle Tom, didn't think you would make it." They shake hands and don't release them as they speak to each other.

"Didn't think I would be invited, but Finn was always the softest." There's a strain in the conversation, and when I glance around the table, Matt is looking at me and gives me a soft smile.

"Sorry to hear about your son."

"You weren't sorry enough to come to the funeral." Their words are delivered quickly. Darragh releases his uncle's hand.

"I didn't think we would be wanted," Darragh fires back and faces me. The strain in his shoulders and around his eyes has me standing.

"Let's check out the room," I say, getting up.

I don't like leaving Ava alone. "Want to come take a look at our room?" I ask her.

"Don't worry, we don't bite." Tom speaks up, but I ignore him and focus on Ava.

"No, I'm good. Just going to find Connor." She uses the moment to stand, and I'm relieved that I'm not leaving her with them. Right now, Tom seems so hostile.

As we leave the main room, Darragh doesn't look up from his phone. His fingers race across the keys.

"Is everything okay?" I ask as we climb the stairs.

He finally looks up and stuffs the phone into his pocket. "Yeah. Sorry about that. So you want to take a look at our room?"

"Just a look." I take a peek at him and he's grinning.

Our room is huge, like stupid huge. The four-poster bed dominates the room, along with the claw bath that sits in the middle of the room.

"Well, a bath is out of the question," I saym running my hand along the off-white ceramic.

"I won't look. Promise."

I laugh at Darragh.

"I promise." He does a little cross over his heart, and I shake my head at him, but I can't stop smiling.

The windows drop to the floor, and I step closer. We're overlooking a garden that's filled with guests, and beyond that, fields and even further out is a forest.

"It's stunning," I say as heat against my back has me catching my breath.

"Not as stunning as you," Darragh whispers into my ear.

I'm so tempted to turn and look at him, but I'm just not that brave. The heat is replaced with cold as he walks away from me. His footsteps are cushioned on the luxury beige carpet under our feet. I stay in the window for a little while longer before I gather some courage and turn around. Darragh's sitting on a clawed legged chair, watching me. My breath swirls and stills in my chest.

"Why are you looking at me like that?" My breath seems shallow as Darragh rises without answering me and steps toward me. I want to fidget or look away as he continues his walk to me. He stops, leaving only inches between us. His eyes flicker to my lips.

"I've never met anyone like you. I've never met anyone who's made me feel like this."

I wet my lips at his words. "What way do I make you feel?" I can't look away from his lips.

"Content. I've never felt that before. I'm always chasing something I can't reach, but with you, I don't mind standing still."

My lips touch his. His surprise lasts only a few seconds before he returns the kiss. We're moving, and soon, the bed sinks around my back.

Darragh moves his tongue into my mouth, his excitement brushing against me, and wetness starts to pool between my legs. Breaking the kiss gives me a moment to think clearly. Darragh trails kisses down my neck, and when he kisses my breasts and runs his tongue across my nipple, I stop him. My halter dress is untied. I didn't even notice him undoing it.

"We need to stop," I say.

He stands with his hands in the air. "I've stopped." He says each word a little breathlessly.

I sit up and hold the dress in place before retying it.

"You started it this time, not me."

I nod while trying to compose myself. "I know I did," I answer as I run my hands across my hair.

Darragh sits on his hunkers so he can see me as I duck my head. "You sound upset."

I shake my head. "No, just guys like you don't normally like girls like me." I'm honest with him. He's scaring the crap out of me, and I don't scare easily. I've seen so much in my life, and I've been hurt pretty badly, but with Darragh, I'm not sure I'd bounce back.

"You have no idea of your worth." He takes my hand in his. "Let's just go back to the wedding and enjoy ourselves. We don't have to figure out everything right now."

He's right.

"But we could say this is our first date." He starts to rise as he speaks, pulling me with him.

"A real date?"

"Yeah." He grins as he twines our fingers together, and we leave the hotel room. "Like boyfriend and girlfriend kind of date."

"Wow, that escalated quickly," I say. His laughter is husky, and my stomach responds by tightening.

"We could be married by the end of the night."

I glance at Darragh sideways. "At the speed you're going, anything is possible."

We enter the ballroom that's been transformed once again. The lights are dimmed, and candlelight casts most of the light around the room. No one is dancing, but soft music plays out.

Darragh isn't slowing, and the horror of what he's thinking of doing has me trying to pull discreetly away from him.

"I don't dance," I hiss.

Darragh throws a grin over his shoulder. "Neither do I." He twirls me unexpectedly. My dress spreads out around me. My free hand presses against a solid chest as Darragh pulls me into him and we are swaying.

"What the hell was that?"

"Just a move I picked up." The heat of his hand in mine is making me forget that we're the only ones on the dance floor.

Glancing down, I try to follow his footing.

"Just let me lead."

When I glance back up, his eyes search my face before landing on my lips.

"Okay," I say. We spin and move around the floor, and I feel like a ballroom dancer. Each twirl has me laughing as I spin, and all the faces merge into a blur. Darragh's smiling face reappears each time as I try to let the dizziness go.

"You're an amazing dancer," I say, trying to catch my breath.

"So are you."

The music softens further, and he pulls me into him until our bodies are flushed. His warm breath brushes my neck. The slow movement allows me to see that we're being watched, and my nerves kick in. Closing my eyes, I bury myself deeper into Darragh and allow myself to enjoy my first dance.

DARRAGH

"Smile, ladies."

Ciara, Una, Ava, and Siobhan are sitting together at a table. They look up and smile as I capture the picture. Looking at it on my phone, Ciara's smiling face and her bright blue eyes have me smiling.

"Let me see." Finn slides in beside me. "Can you send me that?"

I quickly attach it and send it out to each brother. "Sent."

"Are you coming out for a smoke?" I ask Finn, and he nods before giving Siobhan a kiss.

"We're just heading out for a smoke," I say to Ciara. She's watching me, and I want to kiss her but I restrain myself.

"Go. I'm fine here."

I wink at her before heading outside with Finn.

"Where are you going?" Connor falls into step beside us.

"I need a smoke," I say as we head outside. Everyone wants to talk to Finn. So we move into the parking lot, where none of the guests are. I light up a smoke and hand the box and lighter to Connor. He lights up one too and passes the box to Finn.

"It's someday," Connor says and I agree with him.

"Yeah, it's perfect. Just can't believe it's all gone without a hitch. I can't thank you both enough."

"You can take us out for drinks when you get back from the honeymoon," Connor says.

Glancing back at the hotel, I allow myself to relax and enjoy this moment. "Where's the honeymoon, anyway?" I ask.

"A cruise around the world." I'm not much for boats, but a holiday is something I might think about taking soon.

"How are you doing?" Finn asks after a moment of silence.

"Yeah, I was going to ask too." Connor walks over to a cigarette bin and puts out his fag.

"I'm good. It's funny. I feel great," I say to both of them.

Finn smiles. "You look happy," he says.

"I am."

"Do we have to thank Ciara?" Connor's smirk has me nudging him.

"This is all on me," I lie and put out my fag. We go back into the hotel, where the dance floor has filled back up. I spot Shane and Liam drinking together.

"You ever wonder what they talk about?" I ask Connor as Finn gets swallowed up by his guests.

"All the time."

Connor's answer surprises me. I thought it was only me. "Let's go over."

"Don't start anything," I warn and it feels weird. Normally, everyone is warning me. Not the other way around.

Screams start from the side of the room and seem to trickle throughout the crowd. Connor and I pause halfway across the dance floor. I'm searching for the source of panic that's spreading rapidly. Everyone is running as the first shot rings out. I hit the ground hard and cover my head. We're sitting ducks. Connor lands beside me and grabs my arm.

"Move." He's crawling across the floor.

People are running in their panic to get away, and an elderly woman slams into me and hits the floor, the crack of her head making me pausing. The bang of another gunshot has me moving again.

Once we reach the tables, I can't stay down any longer. I need to see what's happening. Standing, I can't see anything through the stampede of people. Climbing onto the table gives me a better view.

"What are you doing?" Connor tries to pull me down. Five men in balaclavas hold shotguns they repump. They're searching the room; they aren't shooting blindly.

A hand grips my leg and pulls my trousers. I see the moment the shooter looks at me. Our eyes meet as he pumps his gun. *I'm going to die.*

Connor's standing, blocking me from the path of the shooter. The gun fires.

CHAPTER NINETEEN

DARRAGH

I'M STARING INTO MY brother's wide eyes. Looking over his shoulder, I see the gunman still staring at us. The screams in the room block out everything else.

"Get down now," Connor warns, and this time, I let him drag me under the table, where a couple and an elderly man are hiding.

"He missed," I say as my eyes roam Connor. He looks away from me. My brain is screaming that he didn't miss. He just didn't shoot us. "They didn't shoot you." I'm rambling.

Connor grabs my arm roughly. "Go find the girls. I'll find Liam and Shane."

Does the shooter know Connor? I'm looking into the eyes of a stranger who shakes me again. "Now is not the time, Darragh."

I pull my arm from his grasp and pause as three more shots ring out. The screams of pure horror are close to me, and I push ahead, one voice striking a chord deep inside me.

Ciara's screams and her cries tear at me, and I no longer crawl. I'm standing, jumping across people and chairs. I halt the moment I see what everyone is screaming for. Siobhan is sprawled out, her dress soaking up the blood that seeps from a bullet wound in her stomach.

She's dead. Ciara is holding her hands over the wound, blood rushing through her fingers. I drop beside them, and Una grows frantic the moment she sees me.

"Oh my God." She's trembling, but I check Siobhan for a pulse that I know won't be there. I spot Ava huddled under a table, her head buried in her knees.

"What do I do?" Ciara's eyes are wild.

I hate that I can't do anything. Shaking my head, Una starts roaring again. It doesn't matter. Everyone seems to be frantic. People are rising slowly, half-bent at the waist.

"Ciara," I take her face in my hands. "She's gone."

Tears trickle from wide blue eyes, and she buries herself in my chest. I'm staring down at Siobhan, her dress rapidly turning red.

"Siobhan!" Finn's voice has me releasing Ciara.

"Just stay here," I tell her before I stand and spot Connor and Finn. I don't see Liam or Shane. Connor meets my eye. His face pales as he stares at my chest. Ciara's bloody hand marks are imprinted on my shirt.

"Are you okay?" Connor reaches me first, and I stand aside.

"Finn." I can't get the words out as he moves closer to me.

"Ah, no. Ah, no." Finn moves past us and falls to his knees beside Siobhan.

Connor looks at me, and I can't hold his stare. I pray to God he had no dealings with this.

"Stay with him," I tell Connor.

Finn is bent over Siobhan, crying as I leave to find Liam and Shane.

"Liam. Shane!"

Arms grip me and I look up into my father's face. "Your brothers?" His fear is gripping him, choking him.

"Finn and Connor are fine. I need to find Liam and Shane."

"I'll help you."

I nod and we both call them. I'm walking toward the last place I saw them sitting. "Siobhan's dead," I mumble to Father.

"Darragh." It's Liam, and he's safe. I embrace him. I want him to fix this. He can fix things.

"Whose blood is on you?" Liam asks, and I can see he's shook.

"Siobhan's."

He nods. "Is everyone okay?"

Father pats him on the arm. "Shane. Where's Shane? He was with you."

"The minute they fired, he raced off, looking for Una." The screams in the room have fallen to cries of despair.

"Shane," I scream again and my voice carries across the room.

"Over here." Uncle Tom is standing, and the strain on his face has me running toward him, with Father and Liam on my heels. *Please God, don't let him be dead.*

There's so much blood. Shane's tie has been removed. I find his pulse and Father is beside me, but he isn't fussing over Shane. "He has a pulse, but it's weak."

"If I find out you had anything to do with this, I will kill you," Father threatens Tom.

"I've been here the whole time."

"Shut the fuck up." My roar silences them. Shane is bleeding to death. Now is not the fucking time. "Someone ring an ambulance."

"I've done it already." Liam joins me, and I move, letting him press his coat to Shane's wound.

"Go be with Finn," Liam tells me and I nod.

I don't want to. I have no idea what to do. Standing up allows me to see the room. It's carnage. The doors open again, and the room is filling with an ambulance crew and the Gardaí. I meet Una near where Siobhan was. Her eyes are red and puffy.

"Have you seen Shane?"

"Una," I say, and she's shaking her head.

"Don't you dare." She's struggling to breathe, her eyes filling with tears. "Don't you dare," she says again, gentler this time.

"He's alive, but he's been shot."

Her hand slaps against her trembling lips. "Where is he?"

I take Una to Shane. The ambulance crews have arrived and lift him onto a stretcher.

"I want him to have the best of care." Father is gripping one of the paramedics by his collar. Two Gardaí put their hands on our Father. Liam and I move at the same time.

"Get your hands off him." I push the closest one back. Gardaí Brady stares at me.

"Don't touch him again," I say and he doesn't speak back.

"Dad, let him go." I pry Father's fingers off the paramedic. "You're delaying them leaving." My words have my father releasing him.

The other Gardaí isn't as quiet as Brady. "Take your hands off me, or I will arrest you."

Liam releases his neck but still stands close to him.

"Liam, come on." I pat his arm, getting him to come away.

"Shane, please stay with me." Una's cries drift away as she leaves with Shane.

"Dad, go with Shane."

Father nods and moves to leave, but the Gardaí that Liam grabbed stops him.

"No one leaves this room."

"This is our family." Liam's composure slips.

"This is a crime scene." The Gardaí moves toward Liam.

"Don't make me arrest you."

"Philips. Leave it." Brady steps in, but Philips is really new to this.

"No."

Una's shouting at the top of the room. They won't let her leave with Shane. I go to join her, but Connor is there, trying to calm her down.

"You will pay for this." Liam's threat is low, but we hear it.

"Turn around and put your hands behind your back." Philips removes the cuffs, but Liam doesn't move.

"I will have your job for this if you don't get him to step away from my son." Father is speaking to Brady, who pales and moves to Philips.

"They just lost family, Philips."

Philips isn't heeding him, and two more Gardaí arrive. Liam raises his hands.

"Fine." Liam turns around, and Philips places his hands in cuffs before patting him down. When he takes his hand out of Liam's pocket, he shows the officers my bag of cocaine.

"That's mine," I say immediately.

"It's mine," Liam barks.

"Possession with intent to sell. You could be looking at a long spell behind bars."

I have no idea what to do. Connor moves toward us, and he doesn't stop as he throws his weight against Philips, taking him to the ground. It's been a long time since I saw Connor fight. All his rage is released as four more Gardaí try to stop him, but he's tearing them down.

"Uncuff him." Father grabs Brady, who pales and uncuffs Liam. The bag of coke is kicked along the floor, and I scoop it up and empty it into a glass of champagne beside us before I join Connor.

I'm throwing punches. My knuckles aren't used to the abuse. Immediately, they crack and I don't stop until I'm pulled off a Gardaí. Connor is restrained too. He did a lot of damage. The Gardaí are rising, but each one has sustained injury.

The room is filling with more Gardaí, and Connor, Liam, and I are pulled to our feet. I'm looking for Finn, guilt churning in my stomach at having left him alone.

"Dad," I call and he moves in front of us. "I'm here with Finn. Don't worry." His words are filled with sorrow. But he gives me a nod.

I'm looking for Ciara but don't see her as we're removed from the room.

A Gardaí van is outside, and we climb in silently. Once the door is closed, I look at Connor. I won't question him in front of Liam, but the fact that he won't meet my eyes makes my theory that the shooter knew him seem more solid.

"It was stupid to attack them." Liam is facing Connor.

"We did it for you." Connor sits forward, but the strain of the handcuffs on his wrists has him sitting back.

"I was getting arrested anyway," Liam fires back.

"Yeah, but I got rid of the coke." I grin at Liam, but he doesn't look pleased.

"That should have never been there in the first place," he says, and I look away this time.

"Poor fucking Finn," I say, not caring about us getting arrested. The charges would be assault, but it was better than Liam going down for possession and intent to distribute. Which was bullshit. There were only a few lines in the bag.

"This will destroy him," I add.

"He will survive."

I look at Liam. "Just once, try not to be so fucking cold."

"You're reckless and emotional. I'm only saying the truth."

"Are you ready for a road trip, boys?" Philips opens the back door. A black eye is already blossoming.

Connor growls at him.

He sneers. "Hold tight, boys, the road is pretty bumpy."

"Motherfucker." I slide off the bench and hit the ground hard. I can't even protect myself from the fall, as my hands are cuffed. When the van finally stops, we're all on the floor.

"I'm going to kill him." I glance at Connor as he tries to sit up. The doors swing open, and Philips smiles at us.

"Everyone okay back here?"

I grin. "Yep. Couldn't be better. How's the eye? Your woman won't like that, now will she?" I hadn't a clue if he was married, but the tightness around his eyes tells me I've hit my mark.

"I bet you're all about missionary. Maybe I need to visit her and really give it to her hard." I get dragged out first, and the concrete floor greets me. Blood fills my mouth, and I spit it out onto Philips's shoes. He dances back, but the damage is done.

"Or maybe your daughter would like my cock." I brace myself for a kick I don't receive. When he kneels down, his grin fills his face.

I spit again. "Sorry, I meant your son." The tightness around his eyes is back as he pulls me up. Two other Gardaí get Connor and Liam out of the van. They aren't manhandled like me.

"It will be a long time before you'll be out of here." Philips moves me to the exit door.

"But the moment I do, I'm going to slip into your son's room."

He doesn't bite but pushes me through the exit and into Navan Gardaí station. I've been booked so many times that I do everything before they ask. Once Philips leaves, I try to get the attention of a female Gardaí.

"Excuse me. I've been assaulted by one of your colleagues. Who do I complain to?"

She glances up at me and raises a brow.

"You can file it with Gardaí Philips. He will be interviewing you."

Fuck.

"But he's the one who assaulted me."

She lets out a heavy breath while pushing my finger into black ink before pressing it against a page.

"You like touching me?" I grin at her, and she releases my hand before looking up at whoever stands behind me.

"Take him to interview room twenty-one." Fingers tighten around my forearm as I'm escorted to the room. The corridor is tight as we pass another Gardaí who's walking in front of Art. I pause when our eyes clash.

Fucking Snitch.

"You okay, man?"

"Yeah, fuckers got me in on an overdue parking fine." I smirk. The Gardaí with Art doesn't comment on him calling them fuckers.

"You need any help?"

"Move along, Mr. O'Reagan." My own Gardaí isn't as patient, but I plant my feet firmly on the ground, refusing to move.

"You don't look like you're in a good position to help me," Art says back, and I want to hurt him.

"I'll be out soon. Don't worry about me. You need anything, just let me know."

The Gardaí have enough of our conversation, and I'm pushed along. I let the Gardaí move me. It's hard to look Art in the eye and not want to hurt him.

I'm left in the interrogation room alone. I want to know how Shane and Finn are. Jesus, Ciara must be terrified. I can't let these thoughts seep into me now. I need a clear head.

The door opens and Philips arrives in with a file. He takes a seat and points at the chair across from him.

"Sit down, Mr. O'Reagan."

I just want this to end.

He's shuffling fucking papers, spreading them out across the table like I'm not here. I want to sit still and not allow him to see my impatience, but I need to get back to my family. I slam my hand down on a piece he's reading. Philips looks up at me and grins. His dark eyes hold a smile. The bruising around his eye is expanding.

"Are you in a rush?" His fingers are perfectly manicured. He's a pencil pusher. I wonder what took him out of the field.

"Nope. Just bored." I lean back in the chair and fold my arms across my chest.

"You assaulted five officers. How do you plead?"

"Not guilty and I don't want to talk to you anymore since you assaulted me. I'll wait for my lawyer."

His lips form a straight line, and he sits back.

"I'm going to be honest with you, Darragh. Can I call you Darragh?"

"Go for it, Philips."

He joins his hands on the table, a move I've seen before. It's making him look relaxed in his delivery of what must be very bad news for me.

"Liam will be released since he didn't assault anyone. The possession charge won't stick since the drugs are missing." He's smiling and I want to smile too, because for me, that's good news. He can get me a lawyer and check on our family.

"Connor, on the other hand, has been released, which is hard to wrap my head around. I can't seem to get answers of why he hasn't been charged with assault."

I don't speak. I have no clue why Connor has been released. He did the most damage. But I don't feel comfort at the idea of him leaving. Especially if he had anything to do with this.

"So Connor knows people, or he's just lucky. But you... You're not so lucky. The five accounts of assault rest on your shoulders."

I stay quiet.

"You see, your family has left you to take the fall."

I glance away, not biting, but the seed of doubt with Connor has already been planted and is growing rapidly.

"Even your friends have betrayed you." I glance at Philips now.

"What do you want?" Everyone wants something. He isn't wasting his time going through this with me unless he wants me to do something.

"Nothing, Mr. O'Reagan. I'm simply informing you of what you're facing. Which is a very long time in prison." He gathers up the pages and puts them back into the file.

"You can't charge me with anything. Where is your evidence?"

He stands and smiles down at me. "Your sister-in-law is dead. Your brother is fighting for his life, and you will soon go to prison. How do you think your family will fare with all this?"

I keep my mouth shut.

"I don't think they'll do so well." He leans in close to me. "One by one, I will take down your family. Paying off the Gardaí will no longer happen."

I grin back. "Let me know how all that turns out for you."

He steps away, but I want to fucking hurt him.

"One thing I know. You won't be able to keep your promise about my family. But I'll keep mine about yours."

The tightness in his shoulders gives me satisfaction as he leaves the interview room.

CHAPTER TWENTY

CIARA

"DRINK THIS." MR. O'REAGAN hands me a glass of brown liquid. It's so cold in the hall that someone has placed a jacket around my shoulders. I can't even remember who.

"Thank you." I take the glass.

Mr. O'Reagan sits beside me. "You saw what happened?" His voice is low as he leans into me.

I meet his eye and nod. My bottom lip trembles, so I take a deep drink of whiskey. "They just shot her."

It was chaotic. We were moving while trying to stay together, and I looked up to see a man pointing a gun in our direction. I froze. I hadn't been able to run or scream like some of the others.

The shooter had hesitated and then pulled the trigger. The bang resounds in my head, and I close my eyes.

"He didn't care." I remember how he reloaded the gun. The red cartridge he'd emptied hit the floor. After all that, all I saw was blood.

"I tried to stop the bleeding." I speak into my glass before finishing it off.

"Did he say anything?"

My shoulders hunch forward. The Gardaí asked me the same questions. I wish I had something to help them. "I'm sorry, Mr. O'Reagan. But that's all I saw."

He pats me gently on the back. My eyes wander to the area still soaked in blood. Siobhan had been removed. Oh God, poor Finn. He was allowed to leave the room with her.

I want to ask about Darragh and Shane, but I don't. No one is allowed to leave the room, so no information is getting in or out. Ava and Una huddle together at a table across from me, both of them still crying.

"Una," I say more to myself.

When the gunman raised his gun, he had been pointing it at Una, but Siobhan moved in front of her and got in the way of the bullet. I saw the slight hesitation in the shooter's stance, but then he'd pulled the trigger anyway.

"It's nothing," I say now.

"No, tell me." Mr. O'Reagan leans in again.

"It's just, the shooter pointed the gun at Una, but Siobhan got in the way. He hesitated like he wasn't sure. But he shot her anyway. I'm sorry. I don't think that makes any difference."

"Maybe it does."

Mr. O'Reagan rises as the door opens, and Liam steps into the room. I'm trying to see if anyone trails behind him, but he's alone. Liam scans the crowd, and his eyes land on his father. He's walking towards u and I stand.

"How's Darragh?" I ask.

Mr. O'Reagan looks at me, but I don't let Liam's gaze go.

"He will be fine, Ciara. He's still being questioned."

Liam walks away and his father follows. I sit back down. Una follows them. "How is he?"

"I don't know. I came straight here."

"Why? He's alone and hurt." Her tears fall faster now. Her hands tighten into fists.

"Go be with Ava," Liam tells her, but she stamps her foot.

"No!" Her voice carries across the room. "You can leave. Go and find out what's happening with him."

Liam is aware that everyone is watching. His eyes flicker across the room quickly before they settle back on Una. This time, I can't hear what's being said. But after some words, Una turns on her heel and returns to Ava.

The Gardaí are still gathering bullets and evidence from around the room. No one is watching the door. I stand and shiver out of the jacket. No one seems to notice me as I move along the wall. My heart pounds when I reach the door. Sweat gathers on my neck and palms quickly.

The doorknob is slick in my hand, but the click sounds like freedom.

The hall is empty as I make it outside. Two Gardaí are outside, but they look at me and say nothing. They must assume I've been let go.

I take out my phone and ring a taxi and ask for them to collect me at Dun na Ri Park. It's only ten minutes from here.

"What are you doing?" I don't stop walking as Liam falls into step beside me.

"I don't know. I just know I can't stay in that room another minute longer."

Liam's fingers touch my bare skin. It's brief, but it makes me stop. "You can't help him right now, Ciara."

"Maybe I just want to go home and wash all this blood off." We stare at each other until Liam finally nods.

"Let me get my car. I'll drop you home. You're better off waiting here and not drawing any more attention to yourself."

Once Liam leaves, I wrap my arms around myself and stay on the side of the road that leads to the gates.

Liam's Bentley rolls down the drive at such a slow pace, like he doesn't have a care in the world. The car slows down beside me, and I get in.

"Are you okay?" I ask him once I've strapped myself in.

He hesitates in answering. "Yes."

He doesn't ask me if I'm okay. "I'm not okay," I say as I watch the green fields and trees pass us.

"I've watched people die. But it was for drugs or money. Watching someone in their wedding dress being shot is unthinkable. And for what? It was meant to be the happiest day of her life." I laugh now.

"It was the happiest day of my life." I can't seem to cry anymore. "Why did someone do that?" I face Liam.

"I don't know." His answer is clipped, and it's the first time I've heard emotion in his words.

"You don't know why someone would hurt your family, or you don't know who did it?"

His eyes slide toward me. "I don't know."

His answer has me sitting back. We pull up into Kingscourt, and the thought of being alone causes my heart to beat rapidly.

"I don't want to be alone," I tell the window as tears blur my vision.

"Unfortunately, I don't have time to sit around and babysit."

My tears dry up quickly, and I get out of Liam's car. I don't have the door closed before he pulls away.

Taking the steps two at a time, I race to my door. My keys jangle in the door from trembling fingers. It takes me several attempts before I get it open. I spill onto the floor, unable to contain the horror of the day.

I wait for the onslaught of tears that seem to rise through my body, but they don't come. Peaches weaves through my arms as I try to hold myself up. I kick out my foot, and the door shuts behind me. The purr of peaches is what I focus on as my stomach roils and reels.

I dig into my bag and remove my phone and dial Darragh's number. Pushing myself up, I lean against the wall as his phone just continues to ring and goes to an automated voicemail.

"Hi," I say. "It's me. Are you okay?" Peaches makes her way onto my lap, and I stare at the ceiling as I speak into the phone. "I'm not. I'm at home now. Call me when you can."

I hang up and sit for a while, trying not to picture Siobhan with a hole in her stomach.

My stomach lifts again, and I rush to my bathroom just in time before I empty the contents of my belly into the toilet. I have to hold on to the toilet bowl as I rise. I don't know the girl I meet in the mirror. There's blood on her chest and neck. My hands have their own coat of blood on them.

Blood that gushed through my fingers as I pressed down on Siobhan's wound.

The blue dress slips to the floor, and I step out of my shoes before shedding my underwear.

No matter how many times I seem to wash my body, more blood twirls down the drain. I close my eyes as I picture his arm hanging over a black sack. That was the first thing I saw. The needle he had used to inject himself with still hung out of his arm. Each step I took further down the alleyway revealed a bit more of my dad. His eyes were still open, devoid of life.

The worst part was, I hadn't tried to perform CPR on him. I sank to the ground across from him and just stared. I didn't want him to live, but seeing his death did something to me. Maybe knowing I was kind of happy he was dead made me feel like such a bad person.

Drops of water make a path down the shower doors. My wriggly fingers touch the moisture as I follow it down and onto the shower tray. I meet it at the bottom as I let the water pour over my head. I sit there until the hot water turns cold and goose bumps coat my body.

I finally get out and wrap myself in a large towel. I turn on the TV and leave it on a random station, as right now I just want the noise. It has someone being interviewed about climate change. I leave that station on and get Peaches some fresh food before returning to my room and getting dressed into trousers and a top.

The buzzer rings and I can't get to it quick enough. It could be Darragh. Maybe he got out.

"Hello?"

"Ciara Michaels." The formal voice has me hesitating. "I'm Gardaí Philips and have a few more questions to ask."

I exhale loudly. "I've answered all your questions."

"This will just take a moment."

I buzz him in. I did leave the hotel when I shouldn't have, so maybe answering his stupid questions will make him leave me alone.

Philips is waiting at the door when I open it. "Miss Michaels, this won't take long." He looks over my shoulder, and I step aside and let him in.

I mute the TV.

"I thought there was a crowd in here."

Folding my arms across my chest, I sit down on my couch.

Philips sits across from me. "You were allowed to leave Cabra Castle?" he asks and I just nod.

"I'm here on a different matter, Miss Michaels. Recently, you were involved in the assault on two men." His words are clear and said with a hidden smirk.

"Yes. But all charges were dropped."

He nods and gives a sharp smile. "I know. The funny part is, I couldn't find the men who had originally pressed charges against you."

I shrug, but my heart starts to pound. "Maybe you need to brush up on your detective skills."

"Hmm." His focus is drawn to Peaches as she saunters into the room and over to me.

"This isn't your first assault case."

"I'm tired and I've just been through a very dramatic day, so really, what is this about?" I rub Peaches.

"What's your involvement with the O'Reagans, besides dating Darragh O'Reagan?"

News travels fast.

"I work for Liam," I answer.

"Cleaning rooms, I believe." Philips doesn't even blink. His brown hair is cut close to his head, like someone you'd see in the army.

"Yes."

"You have no idea what happened to the men who claimed you assaulted them?"

"No."

He nods now.

"Is that all?" I want him out of my home.

"For now."

I can't wait to close the door on him. He has one foot out when he stops and turns back to me.

"I'm not sure if you're very good at playing dumb or if you really have no idea what you got involved in, but if you don't want to end up like Siobhan, I'd advise you to get away from the O'Reagans."

I don't answer him, and he finally leaves. I don't want to think about what he just said, but now it's all I can think about. When I got the call to say the charges were dropped, I assumed Liam had shown them the footage or sent it to the Gardaí station. What if they hurt those men? Killed them? I feel no remorse and that means I don't have a good moral compass to be the judge of this situation.

Picking up my phone, I consider ringing Liam and asking him. Immediately, I change my mind. Now isn't the time. I'm not sure if there ever would be a good time, but now isn't it. Instead, I ring Darragh again. Nothing will have changed, but I just need to make sure. It goes straight to voicemail.

"Hi. It's me again. Hope you're okay. Ring me when you can."

I hang up and sit back down on the couch. I need to do something. Sitting here and ruminating isn't going to help me. After grabbing a pair of runners and my purse, I leave the apartment and ring a taxi.

CHAPTER TWENTY-ONE

DARRAGH

I'VE BEEN LEFT IN this fucking room for the last few hours. No one has come to check on me. When the door finally opens, it's my solicitor, Eric.

"About time," I say.

He sits down across from me. "You're looking at five accounts of assault—"

I wave him off. "Eric, we don't pay you for a recap. Just make this all go away," I tell him.

"I'm trying." His eyes shift around the room, looking for cameras.

The door opens again, and Philips steps in. "Ah, your solicitor finally arrived. We can conduct the interview now."

Eric gets up and sits beside me. "My client won't be answering any questions."

"You don't even know what I'm going to ask. There's no need for such hostility."

"What is my client being charged with?" Eric asks.

"Assault, for now." Philips glances at me before refocusing on Eric.

"And the witnesses?" Eric asks.

Philips leans back in the chair and spreads his hands. "Come on, Eric. I have a room filled with four hundred people. Also, four other Gardaí who were assaulted."

I go to speak, but Eric holds his hand up. "I can tell you now those four hundred people saw the O'Reagans assaulted and intimidated just after the death and shooting of two family members. You used the chaos to assault my client."

Philip's jaw clenches as Eric shuffles some pages and stops on an A4 that has four names.

"Gardaí Brady, Gardaí O'Rourke, Gardaí O'Neill and Gardaí Curran have all dropped assault charges against my clients. So yours just looks false, and frankly, even vindictive."

I want to pat Eric on the back for a job very well done, but I sit still as I watch Philips's case crumble in his hands.

Eric rummages through more paperwork before taking out four sheets. "These are their signed declarations."

Philips doesn't even look down at them. "How can you sleep at night knowing you work for criminals?"

"Very well and on Egyptian cotton," I answer, just to piss Philips off, but he's focusing on Eric.

"When was all this done?"

"When you were seen going through my client's phone and leaving the station. You know it's a criminal offense to touch his property."

"His phone was ringing. I simply answered."

"Who was it?" I ask. I want to know if there was any word on Shane.

Philips smile is sly. "Ciara. She was very upset. So I paid her a little visit."

Eric clamps down on my forearm as I move toward Philips. "He wants a reaction, and right now you're in the clear," Eric informs me.

"Her cat liked me."

I reach across the table and grab both his arms.

"If you do this, Darragh, I can't make it go away." Eric hasn't let me go as he pleads for me to stop. "We are being watched, and there are cameras in the room."

“She was just out of the shower when I arrived.” Philips’s grin is wide.

I want to ram my fist down his throat, but I hear Eric’s rational words and release Philips.

“Can I go now?” I ask.

“Let me go and get your paperwork written up.” Philips leaves and I stand before I punch something.

“He’s trying to get a reaction out of you.”

“Well, it’s fucking working. I want out of here now, Eric.”

Eric gathers his papers.

“Anytime today would be fucking nice.”

He moves faster, and I’m glad to be left alone.

***

I light up a fag the moment I’m out. “Did you bail Connor out?” I ask Eric as we leave the station. It’s dark outside. It’s close to three in the morning now.

“No. Just Liam. I have no idea who bailed him out.” Eric walks to his car.

“Any word on Shane?”

“Sorry, Darragh, but I haven’t heard from anyone.”

I nod as he climbs into his car. I leave the station and walk through Navan. I get out my phone and dial Liam.

“I’m only out now,” I tell him the moment he answers.

“Where are you?”

“Just making my way up to the hospital.”

“You won’t get in. I’ll pick you up in five minutes.”

“Is he awake?” I ask, feeling frustrated.

“No.” Liam hangs up.

I keep walking. I’m walking down the street when his Bentley comes into view. I throw my fag on the ground before I get in.

"Eric sorted it for now, but I don't think Philips is going to let this rest. I have a bad feeling about the guy."

"Right now, we need to focus on Finn."

I rub my face. "How is he?"

"I don't know. I've been helping Eric get you out and also trying to find out how Shane is. He's stable, but he hasn't woken up yet."

"Jesus Christ. Any idea who did this?" I'm so tired. I can barely think straight.

"Not yet. But Ciara said the gunman was aiming at Una, and Siobhan stepped in the way."

"Did Ciara tell you that?" She was that close? My weariness feels like it's seeping into my bones.

"She told Father." Liam drives home.

I don't want to go in. I don't want to look at Finn and what this is doing to him.

"It tells me that the target was Shane and Una, so we need to figure out who Shane has pissed off."

I'm nodding at Liam. He's right.

Every light seems to be on in the house, or maybe that's the fear talking. I was hoping everyone would be asleep. Once I'm out of Liam's car, I spark up and take out my phone.

"You have no new voice messages." I opt in to listen to old ones, and Ciara's voice has me closing my eyes briefly. So Philips had listened to my voice messages.

I don't want to ring her at three in the morning, so I just text.

I'm home now. I hope you're okay. I'll ring you tomorrow.

"Are you coming in?" I hadn't realized Liam was waiting.

"Yeah, I'm just going to finish this." I show him my smoke before inhaling a deep drag.

"I'll be in the library if you need me."

I nod at Liam and he leaves. I light another cigarette up the moment I finish the first one. I'm trying to put off going in. Throwing half a fag on the ground, I finally head inside.

I check the kitchen before heading up stairs. Finn's room is empty, but the lights are on. He was here. His suit is laid out neatly on the bed, his wedding band sitting beside his outfit. Fear has me moving through the house quicker. Liam is in the library, as he said he would be.

"Do you know where he is?" I ask.

"He's in your room."

I nod and leave, not rushing to my room. Why my room? I open the door and have to turn on the lights. Finn's sitting on the ground, a nearly empty bottle of JD dangling from his fingers. His eyes are red and puffy, and when he looks up at me, he squints before drinking from the bottle. I have no clue what to do, so I sit down beside him and light up a fag. He doesn't take the one I offer him.

"I couldn't find drink anywhere. I knew if anyone had some, it was you." Finn's words are sober for a man who has drank nearly an entire bottle of JD.

"Yeah, you never know when you'll need a drink," I say.

"Do you remember the first day we met her?" Finn's smiling.

"Yeah." It's vague, as I was high, but I remember it was at her father's wake.

"Straight away, she captured me." Finn's brows furrow, and he bites his lip before drinking from the bottle. "I wish I could talk to her one more time. You know?" His eyes shimmer as he looks at me.

"I'm sorry, man."

"How beautiful did she look?" His smile wavers.

"She was beautiful."

The cigarette is burning away in my hand. Ashes fall onto the floor, and I brush them away before getting up and putting the fag out in the ashtray on my bedside table. Sitting back down, silence encases us for a moment before Finn speaks.

"I should have never left her side."

"You know that shit will do you no good."

He laughs. "She fucking died on her wedding day." Finn stands and his words grow in sound and power. "Because of fucking me." He hits the bottle against his chest. "I should have left her alone that first day, and she would still be here."

I stand up too. "You don't know that."

"Of course I do!" he roars, causing veins to bulge in his neck. "She was doomed from the moment she met me." Tears trickle down his face.

"This isn't your fault." I'm not good at this. I wish I could be anywhere else. Cleaning toilets in the hotel would be more desirable than watching my brother fall apart.

"I pulled that trigger the moment I fell in love with her." The bottle sails from his hand and smashes against my wall.

I don't move. I wait until he seems calmer. I approach him and take his face in my hands forcing him to look at me. "The best thing you can focus on right now is finding the bastard who killed her and shot our brother."

Finn pulls away from me roughly. "I'm not like you. I don't want revenge. I just want my wife back. But you couldn't possibly understand that."

"Look, you're grieving..."

Finn takes a step toward me. It's frightening what loss can do. I've never seen him look so wild or out of control. Not even when our mother died.

"This isn't grief. It's guilt. I let my guard down with our family, and it cost me my wife." His fist hits his chest as he dances on the spot with anger. "She didn't deserve this." He goes still as his eyes shimmer again and his shoulders fall forward. "She didn't deserve this."

I reach for him, and he doesn't stop me as I pull him into a hug.

"She didn't deserve this," he says again as he starts to cry.

The door opens, and Father walks in. I've never been so happy to see him in my life. He looks like a wreck, as I'm sure we all do.

"How are you, son?"

I step away from Finn so he can talk to him.

"Fine." Finn speaks while looking away and wiping his eyes.

Father looks at me and I shake my head. He sits down on my bed, and I stay standing, not sure if I should leave or stay.

"I remember the day your mother died. I felt like a piece of me died too."

Finn is facing the wall, staring at the broken bottle on the ground. His shoulders shake from silent tears.

"And it did. A piece of me is gone, and I have never gotten it back."

I glance at Father. This isn't helping. Finn turns around and wipes his face.

"I know how wide and empty it is, Finn."

"Does it get easier?" Finn's words are filled with hope and despair, and I want Father to say the right thing this time. Tell him time heals all wounds, and that it will get easier. That he'll find love again.

"Never. Some days it feels even harder."

I sit down at the end of the bed, facing away from both of them, and light up a fag.

"But you learn to live with it. You will live again, but she will always be missing."

I glance at Finn as he cries into his hands. Father stands and places a hand on each of his shoulders. He doesn't pull him into a hug but pats him twice before leaving the room, leaving me with a bigger fucking mess.

"He's wrong," I start.

Finn runs his hands down his face. A spark in his eyes surprises me, and he takes my box of fags and the lighter off my bed. He lights it up and inhales deeply.

"No, he's right. I don't ever want to forget her. I'm also sick of being told that time heals everything. I don't want to heal."

We sit in silence and smoke our fags. The bed dips as Finn rises. "I'm going to try and sleep." He puts out the fag. "I'll clean up the bottle tomorrow. Sorry about that."

"I got it. Don't even worry about it."

There's that awkward moment where I don't want to hug him in case he breaks down again. As I pass him, I touch his back and he nods.

"See you in the morning," he says.

"Yeah, sleep well," I say as I extinguish the fag. Once he's gone, I grab my bin and start to pick up the shards of glass. I don't feel much like sleeping. Ciara has left me a message on my phone.

I'm still awake if you want to ring.

The message was from an hour ago.

Are you still awake?

Her response is immediate. **Yes**

I check on Finn, who seems to be asleep, before I get my car keys and make my way to the library. Father and Liam are still sitting up, both having a drink.

"Finn's asleep. I'm going to go check on Ciara."

"You did good today, Darragh." Father's words have me standing a little straighter. His praise isn't something I'm used to.

Nodding at him, I leave the room.

***

"Can you open the door?" I ask the moment Ciara picks up the phone.

The door lock clicks, and I push it in and climb the stairs to her apartment. She's standing at the door, and her oversized T-shirt and black tracksuit bottoms seem to consume her. She looks tiny and fragile. She's left her blonde hair down, hiding some of her face.

I reach her and pause at the door before pulling her into a hug. Her body shakes in my arms as she starts to cry. My fingers find their way into her hair, and I tuck her closer to me. Her trembles subside and she peeks up.

"You don't have to be here."

"Yes, I do," I say and step into the hall, closing the door behind me. I don't think about it. I just take her by the hand.

"Which room is your bedroom?"

She points to the door on the right. Her place is nice. It's small but clean. Her bed is unmade, the quilts twisted like she's been tossing and turning all night. The lamp on her bedside table is on, and it casts some light into the room.

"Into bed," I say and kick off my boots. She follows my movements as I pull my T-shirt over my head. She swallows.

"We're just going to sleep," I say.

Her wide blue eyes focus on my chest. I open my jeans and let them land on the floor. Ciara still hasn't moved, and I let her take me in as I stand in my boxers.

Her hand is warm as I slip mine into hers, but she pulls away and takes a step back. I'm surprised when she pulls her T-shirt over her head. Her blue bra is full, and I can feel my boxers tighten. When Ciara steps out of the tracksuit bottoms, I'm surprised at the girl who stands before me. She's perfect and sleeping beside her doesn't seem like such a good decision.

I'm considering the couch when she takes a step toward me and slips her hand back into mine. This time, she leads me to her bed and I follow. I lie down and Ciara pulls the blanket over me and lies down beside me. There are a few inches between us, both of us facing the ceiling.

"I think we need to be honest. Neither of us are going to sleep like this." I glance at Ciara, and she faces me now, the blanket tucked under her arms.

"You're right."

I'm surprised once again when Ciara pulls back the blanket and places herself on top of me. She's sitting up on me, and my boxers grow even tighter.

"I'm not complaining here, Ciara. But what are you doing?"

Her eyes seem to devour me, and I rest my hands on her hips. She shivers and closes her eyes briefly.

"I've wanted this for a long time now, and if what happened today has taught me anything, it's that life is too short." Ciara runs her hands up my chest, her face getting closer to mine.

"I've never been with anyone when I'm sober," I confess.

Ciara smiles. "So I'm your first."

I laugh. "That would be a bit of a stretch."

My hands leave her hips, and I grab her face. Her eyes grow wider as she looks at my lips. I move her closer, and she pushes against my chest, stopping my progression.

CHAPTER TWENTY-TWO

CIARA

I'M STARING DOWN AT Darragh, and my heart pounds, threatening to come out of my chest. I'm not normally nervous, and this feels so right. I've played this moment out in my head more times than I care to admit, but having Darragh under me now and knowing how inexperienced I am is making me second-guess myself.

"I... haven't done this much," I say. My heart beats rapidly in my neck, and I'm tempted to touch it and cover it up, but I don't move.

"You don't have to do this." Darragh's words are said softly.

I nod. "I want to."

Closing my eyes briefly, I tell myself I'm not afraid. When I open my eyes, Darragh is waiting, and I answer with a kiss. Being on top of him makes me feel powerful. His body is sculpted and perfect. I push against him, and he groans into my mouth. I deepen the kiss, and a panic takes over me. I want this so badly.

Our kisses grow frantic, and Darragh flips me so I'm on my back. I bite his lip, and he pulls back but grins before kissing me again. Being under him has an entirely different feel. I'm small and desirable. I'm his.

His warm mouth brushes kisses along my throat, his teeth grazing the skin. The pain and pleasure have me pushing against him. I manage to shimmy out from under him, and he grabs me around the waist, but I push his hands away and kneel up. My chest rises and falls as his hungry eyes focus on my breasts.

Reaching back, I remove my bra and let my breasts hang free. I hiss as his mouth covers my nipples. His bites have me digging my nails into his back. Darragh moves back up my neck, and when his lips brush mine, he keeps his eyes open. There's something so personal about watching each other. My hand finds his erection, which grows as my fingers slide over the head of it.

Releasing his cock, I turn away from him and arch my back, cocking my backside in the air. Darragh's large hands grip and squeeze my ass, and pain radiates up my back. Looking at him over my shoulder, I can't wait any longer.

Holding myself up with one arm, I reach back and take his cock, directing it to my opening. He doesn't need any more encouragement. Darragh fills me, and at first, I feel like I'm stretched too far. He eases back out and slowly reenters. Burying my head in the quilt, I groan into my sheets.

"Faster," I plead.

His strong body pulses and pushes against my ass. He grips my hips as he pumps faster and harder.

"Faster." My shouts and groans have his flesh slapping against mine until I release all over his cock.

Darragh trembles behind me as he empties himself, his movements slowing down to a stop. He gives a final two thrusts before pulling out of me. I lie back down, and Darragh flops beside me.

"That was so fucking good."

I'm smiling at his words. "At least you'll remember it," I say, closing my eyes. I'm ready to go to sleep.

"It's not possible to forget you, Ciara."

I open one eye and smile up at him.

"I'm going for a fag." Darragh gets out of the bed and pulls his boxers back up.

"Be careful of Peaches," I say, half-asleep already. The quilts are pulled up on my body, the heat lulling me into a sleep. I've been afraid all night to close my eyes. Each time I do, all I see is Siobhan's empty eyes, the red soaking into the dress. If that didn't haunt me, it was my father's body. I sit up as Darragh arrives back into the room.

"I keep seeing her," I whisper to my fingers. The bed dips as Darragh climbs back in. "I keep seeing my dad too."

Darragh tips my head back so I'm looking at him. "It happens to me."

My lip quivers at his words.

"I allow each face to pass, and then that's it. Don't give them permission to stay." Darragh wipes away a tear.

We lie down and he pulls me into his chest. "I'll keep all the ghosts away, Ciara. You just sleep."

I believe him and allow myself to close my eyes. If anyone can take this away, I know it's Darragh.

***

"I have to go." Words are whispered close to my ear.

"Okay," I say, not wanting to wake up. A soft laugh has me becoming more alert. *Darragh.*

Opening my eyes, I stare up at him. "Morning. Well, is it morning?"

"It's more like dinnertime."

I rub my face and sit up, taking the blankets with me. "How did you sleep?"

"The best sleep ever." Darragh leans in and kisses me softly. "I'll be back later. I'm just going to go to the hospital and see how Shane is."

Guilt rises up. I hadn't even asked about Finn or Shane. "How's Finn?"

The moment I say it, I can see the pain in Darragh's eyes. "He lost someone he loved. Right now, it seems like he'll never be himself again. But with time, he'll be fine."

I take his hand in mine. "He has you, so he will be fine." I kiss Darragh's fingers.

"Can I do anything?" I ask when I look back up at his handsome face. My stomach tightens.

"Keep doing what you did last night, and I'm sure I'll be fine."

I laugh at his answer. "I can do that."

Darragh plants another kiss on my lips. "I better go."

I watch him get dressed, soaking in the perfection of Darragh O'Reagan.

Once he's dressed, he climbs back up and gives me one final kiss. "I'll ring you later."

"Yeah, let me know how Shane is."

"I will."

Once the door closes, I sink further under the quilt and can't stop the smile that coats my face.

DARRAGH

Shane has been moved to the Mater in Dublin. I grab a sandwich and coffee from a deli on the way up. Finn is with me, but he's refused food, and the heavy sunglasses on his face are to help with his hangover and grief.

"Father said Shane woke up last night." Finn stares out the window as he speaks.

"Yeah, I was talking to Liam this morning. So that's good news," I say and glance at Finn. He's still staring out the window.

"I went to your room last night. You weren't there."

Guilt churns away at my stomach. "I went for a walk," I tell him and start to slow down as we enter Dublin.

"All night?"

When I stop in traffic, I look at Finn and see my reflection in his glasses.

"Yeah," I lie and he faces forward.

***

Una is holding Shane's hand. Her back is hunched as I stare in through the large glass window. I want to give them time, but Finn pushes open the door and Una turns to him. The pain on her face is immediate.

Releasing Shane's hand, she walks to Finn and hugs him. I use the moment to slip into the room. Shane's eyes track my movements and I smile.

"You're alive," I say and regret my words straight away as Shane shifts his attention to Finn. "What are the doctors saying?" I try to cover up my previous statement as I sit down on the chair Una vacated.

"I'm lucky. The bullet tore clean through my shoulder. I'll be out soon."

"How are you feeling?" Finn has removed the sunglasses.

Una still keeps an arm around his waist like he might fall down. He looks like he could do with a bed beside Shane.

"Like I got shot," Shane says, and Finn's eyes crinkle at the sides.

"Anyone know who did this?" Shane asks mem and I shake my head.

"I think right now everyone is focusing on your recovery and... Finn's." I say his name low.

"The funeral is in two days. They're releasing her body." Una squeezes Finn's hand as his eyes shimmer.

"Why don't we go get a coffee?" Una smiles up at Finn. I'm so grateful when they leave the room.

"How bad is it?" Shane asks the minute they leave.

"Really fucking bad," I say and rub my face. I feel exhausted again. "Imagine losing Una." I shrug. The thoughts of Ciara being hurt is painful. But loving her, marrying her, and then losing her... I think I would be hell-bent on revenge.

"We need to find out who did this." Shane's jaw is clenched.

"We will, brother. Once we bury Siobhan, we will find out who did this." I'm not sure why I'm telling him this next part, but I feel he should know. "Ciara was standing beside Siobhan when she was shot."

"Is she okay?" Shane asks.

I grin at his false concern. "She will be. She doesn't believe Siobhan was the target."

Something like fear flickers across Shane's face. "What do you mean?"

"She said the gunman was aiming at Una, but Siobhan got in the way."

Shane's pulling himself up, pulling at his drip. I grab it before it falls over.

"Okay, calm down," I tell him before he hurts himself.

"Why am I only hearing this now?"

I sit back down. "Because you've only just woken, Shane. But it does make this look like revenge toward you."

Shane looks away, and my eyes are drawn to the black bands on his arm. I know what they mean, and maybe now one of those bands is coming back to bite him in the ass.

"So who did you piss off?" I grin when he looks at me to try to lighten the mood.

"The wrong kind of people apparently." Shane's face is pale, and I wonder if I should have left this alone until he recovers. "Liam and Father know, so they're on the case."

When Finn and Una return, the conversation is strained, and I decide it's best we leave. The awkwardness isn't helping anyone.

"I'll try to get home tomorrow," Shane tells us.

"No, you will not. You will wait until you're discharged." Una slaps a hand on her hip, and it's so great to watch Shane be schooled.

"Of course, if the doctor says it's fine."

I snort at his lie and he grins at me.

"You need a lift?" I ask Una.

She shakes her head. "I drove up, so I'll stay a few more hours." Una gives me a hug, and I hug her back.

The hug she gives Finn is longer, and I raise an eyebrow at Shane. He shakes his head at me, but I can see the ghost of a smile there.

The drive back feels quicker. "How's Ciara?" Finn asks.

"She's good."

"Is that where you went for a walk last night?" Finn's voice has a touch of humor in it, so I answer honestly.

"Yeah, I stayed the night," I say and glance at Finn.

"You get it on?" I can't see Finn's eyes, as he has the sunglasses back on, but he isn't frowning so I grin.

"I don't kiss and tell."

"I'll take that as a yes." When I glance at him again, he's looking out the window.

"Yes," I say just for him, and when he looks at me, his lip tugs up slightly.

"I'm happy for you, man."

***

The morning of the funeral comes too quickly. Finn insists Siobhan be waked in her own home. The irony isn't lost on me as I stand out back looking out on the old cattle sheds.

"What are you doing out here?" Ciara comes over and links her arm with mine.

"I don't know if I ever told you, but me and Finn met Siobhan at her father's wake. In fact, she was standing right here when we first saw her." I think back to that day and how insensitive I was to her. But all I wanted was to close the deal for Father and get drunk or high afterward.

"No, I didn't know that."

I glance down at Ciara. "It feels like a lifetime ago. I didn't ever think I would stand where she stood, only it wouldn't be her father in the coffin but her."

Ciara squeezes my arm. "We never know when our time is up."

"I know that."

"Do you remember that day?" Finn's voice startles me, and this is a memory I don't want him to have. I nod. He's smiling.

"The moment I set eyes on her, I thought she was so beautiful. I just never thought I would be so lucky to marry her." Finn comes closer. "You were an asshole to her," he tells me, and the fire in his eyes has me holding his stare.

"I know," I say. Ciara seems to be clutching me tighter. "But I made you look good. Otherwise, she could have fallen for me if I was nice."

Finn smirks at my words. "I highly doubt it."

Ciara relaxes beside me.

"I was wondering where you went." Shane arrives, his arm still in a sling. It's a relief to see him up and walking.

"Just needed some fresh air," I say. And some alone time. Which is something I'm not going to get today.

"I'll just see if the ladies need a hand in the kitchen." I plant a kiss on Ciara's head as she leaves.

"She's too good for you." Finn speaks the moment she's gone. His anger isn't like him, but for now, I'll let him say what he wants.

"I know."

Shane squeezes Finn's shoulder. "All our women are too good for us."

When I light a smoke, Shane and Finn take one each.

"No one told me we were having a meeting."

I grin at Connor as he saunters over to us and throws his arm across Finn's shoulder. He's been avoiding me the last few days, but once Siobhan is laid to rest, he won't be able to avoid me any longer.

"A smoke?" I offer and he takes it too.

"I feel bad now. Think someone should tell Liam?" Shane says, and we all say no together.

"I'm glad you all feel that way." Liam materializes and walks toward us with his hands in his pockets. I offer him a smoke and he declines.

"We were messing," Shane says to Liam, who focuses on Finn.

"She has a beautiful home." Finn frowns but thanks Liam. There's that part of all of us that doesn't know what the hell to say. We're afraid to make it worse by saying the wrong thing.

"So what brought everyone out here?" Liam asks.

I notice how we're all standing in a circle, all smoking except for Liam.

"I came out here to have a moment alone," I tell Liam.

Connor smirks at me. "That looks like it turned out well."

"I came out here because this was the first place I saw Siobhan." Finn's looking at me, that same anger in his eyes. "It was her father's wake."

"I saw you from the kitchen and thought a smoke would be nice." Shane looks from me to Finn, picking up on his hostility.

"Ciara told me you were out here," Connor tells me.

I can imagine what she really said. She doesn't like Finn being mad at me, and I've told her how close me and Finn are to Connor. I nod at him and throw my fag on the ground.

"I came out because they're closing the coffin. It's time." Liam's words are like a bomb. We knew it was close, but for Finn, this is it. His final time to say goodbye to Siobhan.

CHAPTER TWENTY-THREE

DARRAGH

THE FUNERAL IS BEING held in Kells church, the same one they got married in only a few days ago.

We all carry Siobhan up the aisle. Finn and Liam take the lead, Connor and I are at the back, and Father and Shane are in the center. The walk feels so long. I can't imagine how Finn is feeling. The idea that this will end soon is the only thing that's getting me through the funeral.

Once we rest her coffin on the stand, we sit in the front row. I don't listen to the priest. I'm stuck thinking about our mother. I have no memory of her funeral or her wake. I have no idea what they buried her in or what prayers were said over her coffin. I wonder now if I was even present, and if I was, did I cry?

I look around me, wondering if all these people stood at my mother's grave. No matter how hard I try to imagine her funeral, I just can't. Bells ring and I look up as the priest moves behind Siobhan's coffin as the two hearse men push it down the aisle. We fall in behind them. Outside, a black carriage awaits her coffin, with two black horses ready to pull it.

They slide the coffin into the back of the hearse. The silence is eerie. The only disturbance is the church bells ringing.

Even the traffic seems to be at a standstill. I can see why now. Gardaí cars have stopped the traffic, allowing us the full use of the road. No doubt bought and paid for.

Ciara walks beside me as we follow the hearse to the graveyard. Her arm links with mine, and I twine our fingers together. No one speaks as we walk the fifteen minutes to the graveyard where Siobhan will be laid to rest.

When her coffin is lowered into the ground, Finn starts to cry, Connor steps forward, placing an arm around his shoulder.

"Raglan Road" is sung, with just a tin whistle accompanying it. I swallow down my own emotion as Finn clings to Connor. Liam, Father, and Shane stand firmly together.

Once the first shovel of clay is put on Siobhan's coffin, the crowd starts to leave and make their way back to Headfort Arms Hotel, where food awaits them. None of us are going. We can't risk our family being targeted again.

I spot Art, DJ, and Fitz in the crowd. DJ gives me a nod when our eyes collide. Today, I don't want to see them. But I nod back. They're a reminder of what I must face soon. Standing here with my family and Ciara reminds me that I'll sacrifice every one of them so I can stay here. I look away and step closer to my family. Una and Ava have joined us. Mary stands off to the left alone.

"I'll be a minute," I whisper to Ciara and release her hand. Mary looks up as I walk over to her. Her smile wobbles, and she pulls me into a hug.

"I'm so sorry, Darragh." Her words are low, even though the funeral is over and most people have left.

"Me too," I say and kiss her on the cheek. "Come over with us."

She shakes her head. "Stephen is taking me back to the house. We will prepare a meal for the family."

I nod and give her a final kiss on the cheek. "That sounds great," I say. "Mary." I stop her from leaving and step closer. "Was I at my mother's funeral?" I feel stupid asking.

Mary looks sad as she touches my face. "You were there but not present."

"Like I was drunk?" I question.

She frowns. "No. You were medicated. You weren't doing so well."

I nod now and Mary leaves.

I return to Ciara and we stand for a while longer before Dad tells us to make our way back to the house. I leave with Ciara, and the minute I'm in my car, I light a fag.

"That was fucking torture," I tell the roof.

She squeezes my leg. "The worst is over."

I look over at Ciara as I lean my head back on the headrest. "Thank you for being there."

She moves closer, her hand leaving my leg and touching my chest. "Of course I'm here. There's nowhere else I'd rather be than with you."

She's looking at me differently and I move closer. The kiss she plants on my lips is featherlight, and she lingers there. "I love you."

Her breath brushes my lips quickly. I lean out to look at her, but she's focused on my lips. Tilting her head back, I make her look at me.

"No one has ever said that to me before," I whisper. "I never really thought about how that would feel." My fingers brush her cheeks. "It feels good." I smile and she mirrors it. "It feels really good," I add before kissing her.

Shane and Una move past my car and get into Shane's.

"We better go." Ciara is still smiling. She's not angry that I didn't say it back, and it makes me want to say it to her. I've never told anyone I love them, apart from my mother.

Ciara leans out and puts on her seat belt. I do the same and start the car.

"I know you met my family at the wedding, but coming to our home is going to be a bit different." I try to say my words carefully without scaring the shit out of her.

"Okay." I can hear the smile in her voice.

"It's only family, so it's small and anything is liable to happen."

Ciara nods.

"I hope you're still smiling when you leave."

She laughs. "The idea of getting to see your home, and maybe your room, outweighs any uncomfortable thoughts I may have."

"My room?" I grin at her. That's one place I would make sure to show her. I cleaned it this morning to have it ready for her.

"Only if you want to." Her shy response has me reaching out and taking her hand.

"That's the only thing that has been keeping me going," I tell her honestly. "Picturing you naked on my bed, screaming out my name."

Ciara laughs while retracting her hand. "We will see."

I grin at her response. "Yeah, we will. You want to bet on it?" I ask her as we drive through Nobber. My stomach tightens as we get closer to home. I hope my family doesn't make an absolute ass out of me.

"I already owe you a grand, so all bets are off the table."

"When are you going to cough it up?" I glance at her.

She's grinning. "I suppose I could pay you with IOUs."

"You mean sexual favors? That sounds good to me."

Ciara's hand slips between my legs, and I nearly lose control of the wheel.

"That's not a good decision." I relax into her touch. "Or maybe it is." She moves her hand in a circular motion. "Should I pull over?"

Ciara removes her hand. "No. Keep driving."

I'm looking at her and taking quick peeks at the road. "Why are you stopping?" My erection wants her back.

"It was just a taste." She smiles at me sweetly.

"You're a tease."

"Maybe I am."

I rearrange myself as we come close to my house. The gates normally open with a clicker on our arrival, but Father had it disabled. The new gate man who is stationed outside the gate in a small booth peers out. Rolling down the window, I try to make his job easier for him.

"It's me. Darragh."

He hesitates.

Ciara sniggers beside me. "Maybe we have the wrong house."

The gates are open, and I salute the new guy as we move up the drive. Ciara is silent and I take a look at her. She's wide eyed, staring up at the house.

"Impressive, isn't it?" I say, looking at it through her eyes.

"It's like right out of a fairy tale."

I snort. "Or a horror movie."

Thankfully, Father didn't alter the garage doors, and they rise as I pull my car inside.

Once the car grows silent, I turn to Ciara. "Okay, we might need a safe word."

"For sex?" Her question is said so genuinely that I can't stop the laugh that bubbles from my lips.

"No, for my family. But a safe word in sex never hurt anyone."

Color blossoms in her cheeks. "What about peaches?"

"Your cat? What if you're just talking about your cat?"

She nods. "De De."

"De De?"

"Yes. De De. It's easy to remember."

I'm not exactly convinced, but I don't want to be late for the meal. "Fine, De De is our safe word. If you need to get out of the room or are really uncomfortable, just say De De."

Ciara leans in with a slow smile burning across her face. "We still need to think of one for the bedroom."

"You look so innocent," I say, holding her face, and she smiles wide now as I plant a kiss on her cheek.

"We better go in."

I'm nervous as we leave the safety of the garage. I want to hold Ciara's hand, but I also don't want to remind Finn how alone he is in the world right now. I find everyone except Liam in the dining room.

Una smiles up at me and Ciara as we enter and pats the seat beside her. I let Ciara slide in, and I sit next to her. Connor and Ava are across from Shane and Una, while Finn and an empty chair are across from me and Ciara. Father arrives and smiles at each of us. Liam follows behind and sits beside Finn.

"I love your dress," Una whispers to Ciara, but with the silence in the room, we all hear.

"Thank you. Yours is pretty too." Ciara sips water and looks around the table. My hand rests gently on her leg that keeps rocking. She's nervous and I don't blame her. This isn't your normal funeral.

Father rises with a glass in hand, and we all reach for the glasses that are placed in front of us.

"To Siobhan O'Reagan. She will always be remembered as one of us. We will live for her and remember her in happy times." Father takes a drink, and we all follow suit.

Finn looks up and nods at Father. It doesn't matter how Finn really feels once Father is around.; he will put on a show. And maybe that's not a bad thing to force him to do.

Shane stands now. "Siobhan was a lady, and I was happy to call her my sister-in-law."

We drink to his words. Good job it's just water, or we'd all be pissed. Una says nice words about Siobhan, as they were close. Ciara remarks on her beauty, and now it's my turn.

"Siobhan had great intuition. She hated me." That gets a snort out of Finn. "From what I knew of her, she was strong, honest, and loved my brother. To Siobhan."

We drink to that and Connor stands. "Siobhan had a great sense of humor and the patience of a saint, with our family as well."

A ghost of a smile crosses Finn's face. Ava says all the right things also, and Una's in tears across the table. I once again touch Ciara's leg that keeps rocking. I want to tell her this awkwardness is nearly over. The sad reality of it is that we didn't really know Siobhan. We didn't bother getting to know her. I glance at Ava, realizing I've never given her time either.

Liam stands now, with his glass in hand. "Siobhan may be gone to us, but for Finn, she will always be alive within his heart. I hope your memories of her are vivid. I hope her smell still lingers, and remember that one day you will join her. To Finn." Liam drinks, and tears fall silently into Finn's mouth as we drink to him.

When the food arrives, no one is hungry. The talk is so small that I want to scream De De at the top of my lungs. I excuse myself for a smoke and offer Ciara to come with me but she stays.

Outside, a soft rain has started to fall, but I don't mind getting wet. Sitting on the front steps of the house, I light up my fag and loosen my tie. The atmosphere in the room is choking, and I've wanted to drink so much, but now isn't the time. Now that the food is nearly over, maybe we can separate. No one wants to be in that room together.

"I didn't know that Liam was a poet." I grin as Connor sits down and takes a fag.

"Me neither. He had no idea what to say."

"None of us did."

"Maybe it would be nice if we did something together." I glance at Connor.

He raises both eyebrows. "Me and you."

"With Ciara and Ava," I say and crush my fag under my shoe.

"Yeah, I can do that." I sit as Connor finishes his fag.

"Did you get to talk to Liam yet?"

"Yeah, yeah, we spoke at the burial," I say and stand, stuffing my hands into my pockets.

"Don't get all defensive. But tell him today." I nod, knowing Connor is right. I dragged it out long enough. The last thing the family needs is for me to get arrested.

"I will," I say and we head back in. Finn isn't at the table, and neither is Liam or Dad.

"Finn is tired," Una says when we enter.

"I'm going to get changed. You coming?" I ask Ciara and she stands. "Talk to you later."

"Be good," Connor calls after us.

Once we're out of the room, I twine my fingers with Ciara's. It feels weird for her to be here but really good too. Ciara looks all around her as we climb the stairs, and I'm forced to see this house through her eyes. The large winding mahogany stairs wraps around the walls before expanding onto a large landing. The oak floors under us are covered in a long red rug that runs the whole way across the landing. Paintings and mirrors that took three men to hang line the walls. Once I open my room door, Ciara returns her focus to me.

"This place is like a museum. It's amazing. I want a tour."

I remove my jacket. "We could start with a tour of my room," I say, kicking off my shoes. Ciara removes her shoes and moves toward my bed, where she sits cross-legged while taking in every detail of my room.

I pull off my shirt, and her attention snaps to me.

I smirk. "I can leave it off," I say.

She bites her lip. "I think I would like that very much." Her wide blue eyes and loose blonde hair make her look so innocent, yet her words aren't.

Stepping out of my trousers, I move to my chest of drawers.

"This is where I keep all my socks and boxers," I tell her and open a drawer.

"Over here is my mirror." I point before pulling off my socks. "That door leads to my bathroom, and that one to my closet."

"I'm impressed, Darragh. I really am." Ciara hides a laugh behind her hands.

"These are my curtains," I tell her, raising a brow while whipping them closed, and she giggles.

I drop my boxers and stand back up as I approach Ciara, who isn't giggling anymore. "And you're on my bed."

"Will I be punished?"

My erection grows as I crawl to her quickly. "Severely."

Her smile is back as she tugs me down onto my back. She straddles me as she pulls her dress over her head. The black number she's wearing is stunning on her.

"We have to be quick," I tell her between kisses.

"I can be quick," she says before biting my lip.

Ciara takes the lead, brushing her underwear aside and placing me inside her. Her body rocks against mine, and I'm tempted to move her under me, but watching her with her eyes closed as she moves rapidly against me has captured my focus. I let my fingers touch her clit, and her eyes snap open.

"That's so good," she says, and I move my fingers faster as she grinds into me harder.

My own release is so close. I want to grab her hips and drill her down on me, but my fingers work her clit until she's panting and moving faster and harder on my cock. We both release at the same time. Ciara crashes down on top of me, a slight coating of sweat on her face and body.

"You are so hot," I say.

She kisses my chest. "That was good."

We lie in silence for a while. Ciara randomly places kisses on my chest, and I can't stop touching her hair. Her smell is something I'm getting used to. Like when she climbs into my car and I smell it, it makes me happy. She makes me happy. I never thought I would find anyone like her.

"You make me happy," I say, and when she looks up at me, I kiss her softly on the lips.

"You make me happy too."

"I'm addicted to you."

Her laugh fills my room. "I'm not sure I like being your addiction." When she rolls back in, she kisses my shoulder.

"Fine. Fine. I'm using all the wrong words." My heart picks up speed. "I love you." I finally say what I want to say.

Ciara's eyes shimmer as she sits up. "Like for real?" Her lip pulls down like she might cry.

I sit up, my fingers touching her lips. "For real."

Her lips tug up into a smile, and tears fall from her eyes. "I love you too."

Taking her face in my hands, I kiss her. Salty tears flow into our kiss.

We lie back down, and I just hold Ciara. It's been such a long time since I've been this happy. I kiss her head again, and she shuffles in closer to me, her small warm body pressed against mine. I allow myself to close my eyes and just relax.

CHAPTER TWENTY-FOUR

DARRAGH

LATER THAT NIGHT, I slip from the bed and leave Ciara sleeping. For a funeral, the day seemed perfect in one sense, but now I know I need to talk to Liam.

Connor, Shane, Ava, and Una still hang out in the dining room. They're all drinking, and I'm tempted to join them.

"Anyone see Finn?" I ask from the doorframe.

Una frowns now. "He still hasn't come out of his room."

"No one has checked on him?" My question is answered with lots of guilty faces.

"I will." Connor gets up and I'm grateful.

"Anyone see Liam?"

"The last time I spoke to him, he was in the library," Connor says.

I tap the doorframe and head for the library. Connor falls into step beside me.

"Are you going to have that talk?" he asks. We separate at the stairs.

"Yes, so you can stop pestering me about it." I grin as I head toward the library, but it soon leaves my face as I think of the complications of what I'm about to tell Liam. Also, for the first time, I don't want to go to him with a problem for him to fix. I want to help fix it.

Sticking my head in, I'm glad to see Liam alone. He's nursing a glass of brandy.

"How are you holding up?" I feel guilty kicking off with something like that, but launching into the real problem doesn't feel right.

"I'm grateful our family is still here, in one piece. For now anyway." Liam drinks from the glass, and I sit down across from him.

"Yeah, knowing Shane will be okay is a relief."

Liam is watching me. He knows me and I hate this.

"I hate doing this right now, Liam. I really mean that. But I've got myself into a pretty serious mess this time."

A ghost of a smile shadows Liam's face, but it's gone so quickly I wonder if I imagined it. "Don't keep me in suspense."

I grin at Liam. His attitude feels different. "I robbed two bank links with friends of mine. One of them got caught, and now they're all going to give my name up to get immunity."

"How long have you been sitting on this?"

"Not long. It just never felt like the right time. Two of the guys are decent and undecided. But I honestly don't think they will be a problem. It's Art and Mark who are going to sell me out." Art's betrayal still hurts.

Liam nods now. "What is it you want me to do?"

I shift in my seat. "I honestly don't have a clue. I just need you to help me."

"I tried, Darragh, remember? I cut you off and gave you a job. But you decided to rob a bank." Liam finishes his drink, and I look away from him. I've never felt like more of an idiot than I do right now.

"Look, forget it. I got it." I stand and fix my trousers.

"Tell me how you will fix it." Liam sits fully back, his legs crossed. The glass rests on his thigh.

"I'll talk to them, convince them not to do this."

"Okay, and if they agree, what happens then?" Liam asks, and I hold on to the back of the Queen Anne chair.

"We all go down," I say.

"Exactly. So you can't win this one."

"What, you think I should go down for this?" I've done so much bad shit and gotten away with it. I know I deserve punishment, but not now. Not when I'm trying to be better.

"Of course not." The bite in Liam's words surprises me. "We need to remove them."

This is what I expected to happen. My stomach twists and tightens and I nod. "I know. Art and Mark—"

Liam stops me. "All of them except one."

"No, Liam. Fitz and DJ are good people."

"You want to go to prison or not?"

I squeeze the chair in front of me, and Liam repeats his question.

"Of course not. But DJ and Fitz don't deserve to die."

"Only one of them. You decide."

I'm shaking my head. "What happens to the one who lives?" I ask.

Liam finishes the drink. "He'll go down for the robberies. Someone has to pay the price, Darragh."

"I can't do this," I finally say. Hurting Mark and Art is hard enough, but DJ and Fitz too?

"Fine. I'll pick for you." Liam gets up.

I'm holding up my hands. "No. Just give me more time. I'm sure I can talk them out of this."

"You don't seem to be listening. The only way out is with three dead bodies and one in prison."

"I said no." I take a step toward Liam. I'm not strong enough to go up against him, but hurting DJ and Fitz? I can't live with that.

"The moment you stepped into this room and told me, that was the moment the decision was already made for you. I'm being kind and giving you a choice of whom to save. For me, it's simple."

I need to warn them. I can't let this happen.

"So pick one, Darragh." Liam places the glass on the bar. "When I leave this room, the decision will no longer be yours."

Clenching my fists, I close my eyes. "Fitz. Don't hurt Fitz."

Liam doesn't face me but nods. "I'll take care of it," he says before leaving.

I don't have much time. I need to get DJ and Fitz out of this before it all goes south. I still have time to fix this.

I will fix this.

***

HEARTLESS #5 IS AVAILABLE NOW: HERE

IF YOU NEVER WANT TO MISS A NEW RELEASE YOU CAN SIGN UP FOR FREE TO GET A NOTIFICATION HERE

About The Author

When Vi Carter isn't writing contemporary & dark romance books, that feature the mafia, are filled with suspense, and take you on a fast paced ride, you can find her reading her favorite authors, baking, taking photos or watching Netflix.

Married with three children, Vi divides her time between motherhood and all the other hats she wears as an Author.

She has declared herself a coffee & chocolate addict! Do not judge

Social Media Links for Vi Carter

Website

Facebook Reading Group

Facebook Author Page

ACKNOWLEDGEMENTS

I'm very lucky to have such amazing readers and Beta Readers. I want to thank the following Beta Readers who worked with me on this book.

Beta Readers
Sandra Curtin
Emmaline Pearce
Amanda Sheridan
Sherry Dale Fram
Patti Shaw
Dani Winland
Michele Rolfe
Julie Collins

www.ingramcontent.com/pod-product-compliance
Lightning Source LLC
Chambersburg PA
CBHW030754190726
48285CB00003B/854